ST GREGORY OF NYSSA
THE SOUL AND THE RESURRECTION

ST GREGORY OF NYSSA
THE SOUL AND THE RESURRECTION

Translated from the Greek and introduced
by

CATHARINE P. ROTH

ST. VLADIMIR'S SEMINARY PRESS
CRESTWOOD, NY 10707-1699
1993

Library of Congress Cataloging-in-Publication Data
Gregory, of Nyssa, Saint, ca. 335–ca. 394.
    [De anima et resurrectione. English]
    The soul and the resurrection / St. Gregory of Nyssa ; translated from the
Greek and introduced by Catharine P. Roth.
        p.   cm.
    Includes bibliographical references and index.
    ISBN 0-88141-120-5
    1. Soul (Philosophy)—Early works to 1800. 2. Resurrection—Early works
to 1800. I. Roth, Catharine P. II. Title.
BR65.G75D413   1992
236'.8—dc20   92–36384
                                                CIP

ISBN 0–88141–120–5

PRINTED IN THE UNITED STATES OF AMERICA

TABLE OF CONTENTS

INTRODUCTION

In the fourth century AD, Christianity emerged from the catacombs and took its place among the spiritual and intellectual forces of the world. As the new faith spread outside its original Semitic milieu, its adherents had to come to terms with Greek ways of thinking. Some, like Tertullian, rejected pagan philosophy: "What has Athens to do with Jerusalem?"[1] Others attempted to reconcile the accepted world-view of their day with the Christian revelation. Among these was Gregory of Nyssa. One of the major points of disagreement between Christianity and Greek thought was the doctrine of the resurrection. Hence Gregory's *Dialogue on the Soul and the Resurrection* provides an example of the encounter between Christianity and Greek culture. It shows us both how Gregory proceeded to deal with the problems in his own intellectual development and how the Church as a whole worked towards a synthesis of the two traditions.

Gregory came from an aristocratic Christian family of Cappadocia. He and his siblings transferred their political and social distinction to a role of leadership in the Church.[2] His paternal grandmother, Macrina the Elder, had suffered in the persecutions. His father, Basil, an eminent rhetoric teacher at Caesarea, married Emmelia, an orphan who would have preferred celibacy but

1 *The Prescription of Heretics* 7.
2 Biographical sources may be found in the *Life of Macrina* (translated by Virginia Woods Callahan, *Fathers of the Church* vol. 58 [1967]) and in *The Fathers Speak* (translated from the Greek and introduced by Georges A. Barrois [Crestwood, NY: St Vladimir's Seminary Press, 1986]). See also the introduction to *From Glory to Glory: Texts from Gregory of Nyssa's Mystical Writings* (selected and with an introduction by Jean Daniélou, S.J.; translated and edited by Herbert Musurillo, S.J. [Crestwood, NY: St Vladimir's Seminary Press, 1979]).

needed a protector. When she was in labor with her first child, she saw in a dream St Thecla, the associate of St Paul. The child was named Macrina after her grandmother, but kept "Thecla" as a kind of private name, suggesting a vocation to virginity. An engagement was arranged for her. When her fiancé died before the marriage could take place, Macrina refused to accept a second engagement, insisting that she should remain faithful to the first fiancé as to a husband. Presumably she thought that this would be the most effective argument for being allowed to remain single and to pursue her real objective, a life of dedication to God. In any case, her mother must have valued her assistance with the numerous younger children.

Sometime after Emmelia's husband Basil died, Macrina persuaded her to start a little monastic community on the family estate in company with their former serving-women. One of the brothers, Naucratius, lived as a hermit in the vicinity, supporting himself and some others by hunting. When he died in an accident, Macrina encouraged Emmelia to bear her grief bravely. The youngest brother, Peter, born at the time of their father's death, was Macrina's especial care.

While the eldest brother, Basil, was in Athens for the equivalent of a university education, he made friends with Gregory, later bishop of Nazianzus, called "the theologian." Basil and the two Gregories remained friends and co-workers for the rest of their lives, becoming known as the "Cappadocian Fathers." When Basil returned from Athens enthusiastic for humanistic learning, Macrina evidently felt that he was too proud of his secular accomplishments. She succeeded in winning him over to the monastic life (about 357). Eustathius of Sebaste, the organizer of ascetic life in Pontus and Armenia, undoubtedly had some influence as well, although the family preferred not to mention his role after he broke with Basil over the nature of the Holy Spirit.[3] Nevertheless, by acknowledging

3   Grégoire de Nysse, *Vie de Saint Macrine*, ed. P. Maraval, *Sources Chrétiennes* 178 (Paris, 1971), introduction, p. 51-52.

Macrina's authority as he does, Gregory puts her in a class with Augustine's mother Monica as one of the great spiritual mothers of the early church.

Gregory, for his part, had to get his advanced education at home, primarily from Basil. Perhaps the death of their father had resulted in financial limitations. In any case, Gregory seems to have caught Basil's enthusiasm for classical literature and philosophy. Not only his brother's example but also the pagan intellectual atmosphere which prevailed during the reign of Julian the Apostate encouraged Gregory's interest in Greek culture. When Basil took up the ascetic life, Gregory preferred to continue in his secular calling. He married a lady named Theosebeia and took up his father's profession as a rhetorician. He was also a reader in church. Rather than contrasting this fact with his position as a teacher of pagan literature, we should probably suppose that reading in church seemed an appropriate role for a Christian trained in public speaking.

Gregory might well have been happy to remain a teacher of rhetoric and philosophy, but in 370 Basil was named Bishop of Caesarea in Cappadocia. He induced his brother and the other Gregory to let themselves be made bishops at Nyssa and Sasima respectively. Gregory of Nyssa was still married at the time, in accordance with the normal practice of those days. Basil was apparently trying to surround himself with dependable allies and to increase the influence of his see. As a bishop, Gregory must not have been much help to Basil; he had problems with administration, finances, and heretics. The Arians deposed him in 376, but he was later reinstated. He gave more assistance to Basil in his capacity as a writer, by providing theoretical support for Basil's monastic program. One of Gregory's earliest works, *On Virginity*, was written for this purpose. In this treatise, incidentally, he regrets that he has not been able to practice celibacy. We may wonder whether he had really changed his mind about marriage or was merely using a conventionally modest form of expression to address those who were undertaking the "higher" ascetic life.

Basil died on 1 January 379. The *Dialogue on the Soul and the Resurrection* is set just after Basil's death, when Macrina in her turn was mortally ill. A little later, while Gregory was away visiting the diocese of Pontus, he was elected Archbishop of Sebaste. In 381 he and Gregory of Nazianzus attended the Second Ecumenical Council (at Constantinople), where a chief issue was the divinity of the Holy Spirit. Basil had expressed his views on this subject in his treatise *On the Holy Spirit*.[4] Sometime after this, the death of Gregory's wife gave him the opportunity at last to try out the monastic life. A letter of consolation to him from Gregory of Nazianzus speaks with respect and affection of Theosebeia.[5] Why could Gregory of Nyssa praise his virgin sister but not his wife? Was even a married theologian biased toward celibacy? Be that as it may, the last we hear of Gregory is his attendance at a synod in 394. Probably he died soon thereafter.

Gregory's writings fall into several categories. His treatises on Christian doctrine often involve polemics against contemporary heretical teachings. He wrote commentaries on various biblical books. Several of his works deal with the ascetic life. Naturally, the circumstances of his life also required him to deliver sermons on different occasions and to communicate with diverse individuals by letter. These categories are of course not mutually exclusive. His biography of Macrina, for example, takes the form of a letter and offers a model for the monastic life; hence it is usually listed with the ascetic works. Writers of late antiquity often used the epistle form to present an essay on any subject.

Another ancient literary form appears in the *Dialogue on the Soul and the Resurrection*. The choice of a dialogue form shows

4   See Basil the Great, *On the Holy Spirit*, trans. David Anderson
     (Crestwood, NY: St Vladimir's Seminary Press, 1980).
5   *The Fathers Speak*, 215-217.

that Gregory wanted to be recognized as a successor to the tradition of Plato. It has often been pointed out that his dialogue shows many parallels with Plato's *Phaedo*.[6] There is also a relationship with Plato's *Symposium*, where Socrates becomes the not-so-apt pupil of the wise woman teacher Diotima. Gregory similarly makes himself the pupil of his wise older sister, putting the stubborn and foolish questions into his own mouth. Is this merely modesty? Is it an honest depiction of his respect for Macrina's authority? Is it a means of avoiding full responsibility for the conclusions reached? Is it a way for Gregory to portray his own inner conflict, as he struggles to reconcile his Hellenism and his Christianity?[7] In that case it makes sense that Macrina, who led him into an ecclesiastical career, should take the "Christian" part, while Gregory himself, the former teacher of rhetoric, assumes the contrary position. We would like to know how closely the Macrina of the dialogue represents the historical Macrina. It is certainly possible that she was such an educated and reflective woman. If Gregory's own education was acquired chiefly at home, she could have learned as much as he. Unfortunately, we have no other witness to corroborate Gregory's testimony.

Through the dialogue with Macrina, Gregory attempts to present the doctrine of bodily resurrection in terms of the Platonic philosophical tradition, but also in accord with the biblical revelation. Many readers have felt doubts that he succeeded in integrating his philosophy with his Christianity. Harold Cherniss in particular claims that Gregory was a Platonist in his heart, and that he made an intellectually dishonest concession to his overbearing

6   *E.g.* A. M. Akulas, *The opinion of Plato concerning the immortality of the soul in comparison with that of Gregory of Nyssa* (in Greek) (Athens, 1888); P. Wilson-Kastner, "Macrina: Virgin and Teacher," AUSS 17 (1979) 110; Charalambos Apostolopoulos, *Phaedo Christianus* (Frankfurt: Peter Lang, 1986), 6, 13-18.

7   Apostolopoulos, *Phaedo Christianus*, 117.

older sister when he inserted Christian doctrine into his writings.[8]
Charalambos Apostolopoulos considers Gregory to be a Greek
philosopher of notable originality who, because he feared the ecclesiastical authorities, disguised the boldness of his thought with
pious formulas and biblical citations.[9] Indeed, Gregory's contem-
poraries had already accused him of too great fondness for pagan
writers, as a remark of his in *De instituto Christiano* shows.[10] Jean
Daniélou, on the other hand, believes that Gregory's thought is
wholly Christian, though expressed in Platonic terminology.[11] I
suspect that these writers would differ in their understanding of
what the Christian doctrine is with which Gregory's ideas are or are
not compatible. Besides, I venture to suggest that we can look at the
question in another way. We may think of Gregory as an intellectual
who accepted the scientific world-view of his time, much as we
accept relativity, evolution, and the other generally accepted theories of our time. He was also a Christian. Many of us are content to
keep our philosophical and scientific views in a separate mental
compartment from our Christian beliefs. Gregory was not. He
hoped to be able to show, to his own satisfaction and to that of
others, that Christian faith could be intellectually respectable. He
was trying to do for his time what Thomas Aquinas and Teilhard de
Chardin (for instance) have tried to do for their times. We are not
likely to accept the whole system of any of these thinkers, much as
we admire their efforts to create comprehensive theories of the
universe. At the same time, we do not doubt the sincerity of their
Christian faith.

So why was the resurrection a problem? People raised on
Greek modes of thought had difficulty accepting that the body

8   H. F. Cherniss, *The Platonism of Gregory of Nyssa* (Berkeley,
     1930), 57-58.
9   Apostolopoulos, *Phaedo Christianus*, 110-111 *et passim.*
10   *Gregorii Nysseni Opera* 8.1.43.1-7.
11   J. Daniélou, *Platonisme et théologie mystique,* ed. 2 (Paris,
     1953).

would or could be raised. They knew perfectly well that the body decays and disintegrates when a person dies. The Homeric epics (like the earlier phases of the Hebrew tradition) imply that death is the end of personal existence. The "soul" (ψυχή) is a shadowy thing which departs when the person dies; the body is the man himself. Some Greeks had different ideas, however. The so-called "Orphics" and the initiates of certain mystery cults appear to have believed in some kind of immortality, most likely in the form of reincarnation. Influenced by these traditions, Plato taught in the *Phaedo* and the *Republic* that the soul is immaterial and immortal, and that it, rather than the body, is the real person. The wise man aims to free his soul from the influence of the body insofar as he can even before his physical death, so that it will be prepared to live the disembodied heavenly life which lasts for eternity.

The idea of bodily resurrection seems to have arisen in Hellenistic Judaism (the period of the Apocrypha). It was felt that those who had died under persecution must receive their reward at some later time. The belief in resurrection became an issue between the Pharisees and the Sadducees, a fact of which the apostle Paul took advantage (Acts 26). The first Christians were convinced that they had seen Jesus alive after His death. It was from this experience that they developed their doctrine, not from theory (though the Pharisaic belief must have helped them to interpret the experience). When they came to formulate statements of doctrine, they had to fit this intransigent experience into some more-or-less systematic world-view. St Paul encountered people at Corinth who doubted the possibility of resurrection, asking what the resurrection body would be like (1 Cor 15). Paul did not claim to know in detail. He must have taken as his starting point the eye-witness reports which became the sources for the canonical Gospels. We are told that Jesus was able to eat fish after his resurrection; and his body was evidently solid to the touch, though Thomas did not need to try the experiment. At the same time, he was able to appear and disappear at will, even passing through locked doors. From this kind of evidence Paul must have concluded that the resurrection body is in fact material, but that it differs in significant ways from the present body. He compares it to a plant growing from seed, which seems to die before it grows again in a different form, yet remains the same species of plant.

After St Paul, Gregory's most notable predecessor in writing on the subject of the resurrection was Origen of Alexandria. Philo, the Jewish philosopher of the same city, had attempted to interpret the Hebrew tradition according to Greek philosophy. Although his methods, as far as we know, were not accepted by other Jewish thinkers, they had a major influence on Christian thought. Origen, following Philo's example, tried to synthesize Platonism and Christianity. As a pioneer in this project, he was inevitably subjected to criticism. He was accused of teaching that souls, which began along with the angels as bodiless beings, would finally return to incorporeality. We have difficulty knowing exactly what he really said, as we do not have the whole text of his *On First Principles*, only translations and excerpts made by partisans or opponents who all had their own reasons for distorting the evidence. As far as we can tell, however, he suggested the return to incorporeality as a hypothesis (in accordance with his theory that the end would be like the beginning), but inclined to prefer the alternative hypothesis of an ethereal resurrection body. Methodius of Olympus, in opposition to Origen, insisted on the resurrection of a genuinely material body. Gregory attempts to meet Methodius' objections. He rejects the more eccentric aspects of Origen's theories (such as the pre-existence of souls), while preserving the basic idea which Origen holds in common with St Paul, that the resurrection body must be somehow finer, purer, and more splendid than the present body.

Gregory's dialogue begins, like Plato's *Phaedo,* with the concrete situation: how do we face the death of a loved one, or our own death for that matter? In the *Phaedo,* as the time for Socrates' execution approaches, he explains to his friends and disciples how he is convinced that the soul is immortal. Here, while still mourning for his brother Basil's death, Gregory discovers that his sister Macrina is also about to die. As in the *Phaedo*, the dying person must console the survivor.

Macrina asks Gregory what makes him fear death. The heart of the problem seems to be that he lacks confidence in the survival of the soul. He accepts this as an article of faith, but he does not feel convinced. So Macrina proposes a dialogue on the subject of the soul. Gregory's role will be that of "devil's advocate." Suffering as he is from the grief of losing his brother and sister, he will be able to present the objections with genuine feeling, not merely as an intellectual exercise. Indeed, throughout the dialogue, Gregory's emotionalism contrasts with Macrina's calm self-control.

Gregory has already raised the question, "Does the soul survive the death of the body?" Obviously the dead body is dissolved into its elements, as it disintegrates in the earth. In saying "elements," Gregory is referring to earth, water, air, and fire, in accordance with the theory accepted by Greek science; but we may think of molecules if we prefer. Gregory then poses a dilemma. The soul is either material or immaterial. If it is material, it will be dissolved along with the body. If it is immaterial, it cannot be contained in the elements. Everything consists of elements, so there is nowhere else it can be. Therefore, he concludes, the soul does not exist after the death of the body.

In saying that everything consists of elements, Gregory has been tacitly assuming that only material things exist. Macrina replies that if immaterial things do not exist, then two consequences follow: there is no soul even in living bodies, and God does not exist either. But, she says, the order in the universe proves that God exists. Similarly, the activity of reason proves that a soul exists in us. Therefore immaterial things can exist.

Without yet being fully convinced of the soul's existence,

Gregory asks about its nature. What kind of thing is the soul? Macrina provides a definition. She supports her case by referring to the way we make inferences which go beyond our immediate sense-impressions. Gregory concedes the existence of the soul, but still asks for a more positive description of it. Macrina rebukes him, saying that a negative formulation tells us enough. We have to be satisfied with negatives in the case of God, for example. Gregory petulantly objects that this makes the soul the same as God. Macrina replies that the soul is *like* God, but certainly not the *same*. Just as God is in the universe maintaining its existence, so also the soul is in the body giving it life. The soul remains different from the body even while joined with it; consequently, when the body is broken up the soul can still be joined with the elements. Gregory wants to know how the soul can go in different directions when the elements of the body are scattered. Macrina answers that distance and separation have no significance for immaterial things; they affect only bodies.

In considering the nature of the soul, we have to take account of the emotions. We do not just *think*, Gregory says in effect, we also *feel*. Feelings are not part of the body; are they part of the soul? As his tone here becomes somewhat insolent, he receives another reprimand from his sister. Pagan philosophers (such as Plato and Aristotle) talk about the emotions, she says, but we for our part have to rely on the Bible. We must reject Plato, Aristotle, and the Presocratic philosophers—and the science of logic into the bargain. Nevertheless she argues logically from a classical definition of man as the "rational animal." The definition would have mentioned the emotions if they were essential. It did not mention them, so they are not essential. She continues with a further logical argument, this time premised on a scriptural text. If Moses could be without anger and desire, these emotions are inessential; he was meek, therefore anger is inessential. We might feel that this argument puts too much weight on one biblical passage, neglecting other events in Moses' story. The conclusion is conveniently Platonic, reminding us how Plato defended the unity of the soul in the *Republic* (611B). Was the lady protesting too much when she claimed to be rejecting logic and philosophy?

Gregory raises an objection from the Bible. Emotions are praised in various scriptural passages, so they cannot be bad. Macrina clarifies her point: emotions are on the boundary of the soul and can be used well or badly. God cannot have given man any faculties which are wholly evil. In the order of creation, plants came first, with the power of nourishment and growth, then animals with perception and emotion, and finally human beings with reason. Each form of life requires the preceding. Perception is necessary to link intellect with body, so humans acquire emotions along with perception as aspects of animal life. Once again she professes to be presenting a simple narrative based on scripture, but the conclusion is suspiciously reminiscent of pagan philosophy. This time we recognize Aristotle's theory of the vegetable, animal, and rational souls, as set forth in his treatise *On the soul*.

The emotions work for good, Macrina says, if they are controlled by reason. She uses the parable of the tares to support this assertion.The good seeds are our emotional impulses. The bad seeds are errors in our judgment of what is good. It is the mind which misleads the emotions, not *vice versa*. We remember the Socratic principle that virtue is knowledge, that no one does wrong except in ignorance. Macrina seems to insist most firmly on her biblical sources when her argument is most philosophical—that is to say, when Gregory was most vulnerable to criticism from "fundamentalist" opponents.

Gregory accepts this explanation of the emotions. Returning to the subject of what happens to the soul after death, he asks his next question: what is meant by Hades? People generally think that it is a place for the souls of the departed. Macrina replies that, first of all, Hades cannot be on the dark side of the earth, because the earth is a sphere which is illuminated on all sides in turn; and in any case it is not a place, because the souls are incorporeal and do not need to be in a place. Instead, we should understand Hades as a change in the soul's condition. Referring to Philippians 2:10, she interprets the beings in heaven, on earth, and under the earth as angels, humans in this life, and humans after death. The last category might alternatively be understood as demons; this would be Origen's view. All these beings will be united at the end of the present age.

Accepting this interpretation of Hades, Gregory continues with a more difficult question: how can the soul recognize the elements of its body when they are scattered? Macrina tries to explain this by analogy with the mixing of paints, as if paints which are mixed could be unmixed and then mixed again. She does not claim that the unmixing is possible. Her point is rather that when the artist has mixed a certain color once, he knows how to produce the same mixture a second time. In the case of paints, an artist uses an additional supply of the same kinds of pigments. In the case of resurrection, however, the very same elements must be used, or else the result will not be resurrection but a new creation. She draws another analogy: when clay pots are broken up, we can still recognize which of the original pots was the source of each fragment, and we can also tell the difference between unworked clay and potsherds.

The parable of Lazarus and the rich man draws together Gregory's last two questions. It shows, first, that the places of the dead are really states which we have chosen for ourselves. Second, it implies that the soul can recognize not only the elements of the body as a whole but also the elements of each body part. The parable also introduces a new theme, that we need to free ourselves from attachment to fleshly life. This reminds us strongly of Plato's *Phaedo*, except that Plato said "body" rather than "flesh." "Flesh" (σάρξ) is

a Pauline word for the fallen nature of man, including aspects of
soul as well as of body.

This theme inevitably leads to the next question. If emotions
are not an essential part of the soul, but are part of the fleshly life
from which we must detach ourselves, then we must also be freed
from desire. In that case, how can we love God? Macrina replies
that freedom from emotions makes us more similar to God.
According to the old Greek principle that like is drawn to like, we
will be more strongly attracted to God as we become more like
Him. We do not need *desire* when we reach the goal, but we can
still *love*. Desire (ἐπιθυμία) reaches out for the unattained (as
ἔρως does also). Love (ἀγάπη) can be an enjoyment of what we
have. When the lovable object is infinite, love can be infinite also.

While they are on the subject of purification, Macrina must
deal with the question, "Why is our purification painful?" She
says that the pain comes because we need to be separated from
impure accretions. The more evil we have allowed to grow onto
us, the more pain we will endure as it is pulled away. Finally,
however, we will be completely liberated from evil. When all our
voluntary choice is brought into God—when God is "all in all,"[12]
evil will no longer exist. Evil is a privation of good; it does not
exist by its own nature, only by our choice. So the purificatory
suffering must end when this age ends, when all things are restored to their original condition. In fact there is no Hell properly
speaking, only a kind of Purgatory. Needless to say, the denial of
eternal punishment was one of Gregory's (and Origen's) more
controversial ideas.

For Gregory, it is bad enough that some people will have to
suffer for the whole duration of the present age, not to say forever.
He wonders how a person can face the prospect of even that much
suffering. Macrina first gives the practical advice that one should
avoid evil, and thus not have so much to endure. She adds

12 1 Corinthians 15:28.

scriptural argument for the the belief that evil will finally be anni-hilated. When Gregory asks how we should console people who are suffering now, Macrina assures him that their future reward will be much greater than their present suffering. Once we are cleansed, she says, we can grow without limit in the capacity for good. Besides, even our bodies will be returned to us in a purified condition.

At this point the dialogue is ready to deal with the resurrection itself. How can it happen? We accept it as a scriptural doctrine, Gregory says, but we fail to understand it. Macrina's answer has three parts. First, she discusses pagan ideas which have some similarity to the Christian doctrine of the resurrection. Second, she considers the genesis of the soul, how it is related in time to that of the body. Finally, she meets objections to the doctrine of the resurrection.

First, she says, the various theories of transmigration show that some pagans have believed in a return to bodily life. They are correct in thinking that the soul can live again in a body; but they are wrong to suppose that the soul returns in a different body from the one it had before, whether human or otherwise. Against the belief that human souls can be incarnated in non-human bodies, she asserts that human souls are different from animal and vegetable souls. This was Aristotle's teaching in his treatise *On the soul*. Each kind of soul needs to have the right kind of body.[13] In contradiction to the idea that souls go through cycles of reincarna-tion, she ridicules the notion that souls in heaven would become bad while embodied souls on earth become good. Heaven is normally supposed to be the good condition, and material life inferior. Fur-thermore, she says, if evil were the beginning of our human life, we could never become good. If chance were the beginning, we could never rely on Providence. The word "beginning" (ἀρχή) includes the idea of "principle," so whatever does not occur at least poten-tially in the beginning cannot develop later on. But in fact virtue does

13 Aristotle, *On the soul*, 407b, 22-26.

occur. Therefore it cannot be evil which begins our life, so it must be God who is responsible for our origin. Virtue is natural to us; evil is a defect in our nature, occurring either by our choice or by some kind of disease.

If the theories of transmigration cannot account plausibly for the entrance of souls into bodies, then how and when does the soul come into its body? Although Macrina says that we cannot know *how*, she does still venture a few remarks on creation. We can readily accept that the immaterial God creates incorporeal souls, but how can He create matter? Matter comes neither from God's nature nor from any other source besides God. Actually matter is not really material, but a combination of qualities. These God can easily create. After this digression, Macrina returns to the question of *when*. If souls were created *before* bodies, we would have the same difficulty in explaining how they entered bodies as we had on the assumption of transmigration. If souls were created *after* bodies, the bodies would not be alive before they had souls, since the soul is (among other things) the principle of life. But everyone knows that the fetus in the womb is alive, because it grows and moves. So body and soul must arise at the same time. Macrina makes a final point concerning the creation of bodies and souls: the process will eventually cease, when the number of human beings is complete.

Now Gregory hopes to bring up the objections which are raised against the doctrine of resurrection. Macrina, however, prefers to start with the scriptural testimonies: the Psalms, Ezekiel, and the New Testament. After she goes through all this at considerable length, Gregory reiterates his question, adding vivid, not to say repulsive, details. Many difficulties arise, he says, when we try to imagine what the resurrection will be like. If our bodies die of disease or injury, will we rise with defective bodies? Our bodies change during our life; will we rise with a young or an old body? If we sin and repent, how can the sinful body be punished and the repentant body be rewarded? Given that we will not marry or eat in the resurrection, do we rise with or without our reproductive and alimentary organs? If we rise *with* them, God will have made something useless. If we rise *without* them, how can our resurrection body be the *same* as our present body?

Macrina rebukes this rhetorical outpouring, telling Gregory that he has missed the point. Resurrection, she says, is the restoration (ἀποκατάστασις) of our nature to its original condition. The original condition in paradise was free from evil and passion, from alimentation and reproduction, from birth, growth, old age, and death. All of these belong to the "garments of skin" which Adam and Eve received after the Fall. Parenthetically we may ask how this description of the original condition is consistent with Macrina's earlier version of man's creation, in which he was created by God as the summation of vegetable and animal life. Was that after all not the first creation, but a re-creation after the Fall, when the "garments of skin" were acquired? That was not the impression we received when we were reading that passage. In any case, Macrina now says that the resurrection body will have none of the transitory characteristics which go with the bodily functions.

Furthermore, everyone will be raised. Good people will attain blessedness sooner, evil people will require longer purification. As for Gregory's objections, St Paul has already answered them in speaking of the seed and the plant, and of the corruptible which puts on incorruption (1 Corinthians 15). Besides, if in Genesis the plant was created before the seed, we should understand that death comes before new growth. At the end of this age, all of us will finally be restored to God's likeness.

To summarize the whole dialogue briefly: the soul exists and is immaterial and imperishable. It is attached once and for all to the elements of a body. When the elements are scattered, the soul remains in contact with them. Emotions, while not evil in themselves, are inessential to the soul. We must be purified from the fleshly aspects of our life, including the emotions. We will still be able to love God, because that kind of love is an attraction of like to like. Our purification is likely to be painful, because evils have adhered so closely to us, but it will end at least by the conclusion of the present age. At that time we will all be restored to our bodies. These bodies will be made from the same elements as before, but assembled in a new way, or rather in the way they would have been before the Fall.

What does this argument have to do with us? We will probably not be convinced by the idea that the very same molecules must be brought back together to constitute our resurrected body. We are too much aware that the elementary particles of our matter go through many changes and recombinations—but the ancients knew that too. They thought, for example, about the possibility of a fish eating a drowned person and then being caught and eaten by another human being.[14] On the other hand, our science fiction makes us familiar with the idea that our molecules might be taken apart and put back together: "Beam me up, Scotty!"[15] Basically, we should probably accept Gregory's affirmation that our whole being, body and soul, will return to life, in continuity with our present person but with greater wholeness. We are not likely to commit ourselves to any particular theory of how this takes place. Perhaps we will wish to follow up the suggestion that matter is not really material, since we have discovered that matter and energy are interchangeable. Gregory did not venture to explore the full

14 J. Daniélou, "La résurrection des corps chez Grégoire de Nysse," *Vigiliae Christianae* 7 (1953) 163.

15 For a light-hearted discussion of the issue, see Dorothy Derifield, "The Perils of the Future," *Radcliffe Quarterly*, vol. 77, no. 1 (March 1991) 30: "...it seems to me that rather than beaming actual molecules from place to place, it makes more sense to beam just the pattern, since the molecules I'm made of are readily available. In other words, 'Fax me up, Scotty.' This could lead to many interesting complications, not the least controversy over what happens to the soul during the beaming process."

implications of his idea, which would probably have been too dangerous for him to publish: what could it mean for the corporeality of the resurrection body? Would we choose to imagine that the resurrection body is more like energy than like matter? Just as Gregory based his speculations on the science of his time, so we also are free to make our guesses in accord with the theories of our time, realizing that our conjectures, like his, will undoubtedly be superseded. New theories will lead to new guesses, and finally the reality will invalidate all speculations. As Macrina said,

> The truth about this is stored up in the hidden treasury of wisdom and will be disclosed at the time when we are taught the mystery of the resurrection in deed, when we will no longer need words to reveal what we hope for. If at night wakeful people discuss at length what the light of the sun is like, the grace of the rays by its mere appearance makes vain the verbal description; in the same way every reasoning which conjectures about the future restoration will be proved worthless when what we expect comes to us in experience.[16]

This translation has been made from the text of Krabinger (1837).[17] The dialogue is also found in Migne's *Patrologia Graeca*, volume 46, columns 11-160; it is not yet available in either the critical edition of Gregory's works begun by Werner Jaeger or the French series *Sources Chrétiennes*. While I was in the United States I consulted the translation by Virginia Woods Callahan.[18] Her version was helpful in some of the difficult spots; in others I have ventured to disagree with her. Since I have been living in Germany, although benefiting from the admirable collection of the University of Trier, I have no longer had access to her translation. In the

16 Below p. 113.
17 *S. Gregorii eposcopi Nysseni De anima et resurrectione cum sorore sua Macrina dialogus,* ed. J. G. Krabinger (Leipzig, 1837).
18 Saint Gregory of Nyssa, *Ascetical Works,* translated by Virginia Woods Callahan, *Fathers of the Church* vol. 46 (Washington, 1967).

summer of 1989 I had the privilege of participating in a summer
seminar sponsored by the National Endowment for the Humani-
ties and directed by Professor Louis Feldman of Yeshiva University. This seminar allowed me to investigate some of the biblical
and Greek sources of Gregory's thought in an atmosphere of
intellectual challenge and scholarly fellowship.[19] In preparing this
translation for publication, I have had the assistance of Professor
Paul Meyendorff of St Vladimir's Theological Seminary. A spe-
cial debt of gratitude to Professor Jaroslav Pelikan, for suggesting
the idea of this translation to St Vladimir's Seminary Press. My
husband, Father Gregory, enjoys arguing with me over the theory
and practice of Greek patristric translation, and our children
Nathaniel and Margaret have tolerated their parents' peculiar
form of recreation.

Catharine P. Roth
Steinwenden, Germany
19 July 1991
Feast of Saint Macrina

---

19 Seminar paper published as "Platonic and Pauline Elements in
    the Ascent of the Soul in Gregory of Nyssa's *Dialogue on the
    Soul and the Resurrection," Vigiliae Christianae 46 (1992)*
    20-30.

CHAPTER 1

The Survival of the Soul

When Basil, the great saint, had passed over to God from the life of men, he gave the churches a common cause for grief.[1] As our sister and teacher still remained in this life, I went in haste to share with her the sad news concerning our brother. My heart was very sorrowful for grief at so great a loss, and I sought to share my tears with someone who would bear an equal burden of anguish. But as we came in sight of each other, the appearance of my teacher stirred up new suffering for me, for she also was already afflicted with a mortal illness. She, however, like an expert equestrian, allowed me to be carried away briefly by the momentum of my grief, then tried to rein me in with her words, using her own reasoning like a bit to correct the indiscipline of my soul. She reproached me with the apostolic saying, that we should not grieve concerning those who are asleep, because this emotion belongs only to those who have no hope.[2]

My heart was still overflowing with grief. "How can we human beings accomplish this," I asked, "since there is naturally such a strong aversion for death in each one of us? When we see those who are dying, we do not easily accept the sight; and when death approaches, we flee from it, as much as we are able. Besides, the prevailing laws judge death to be both the greatest crime and the greatest punishment. How, then, can we consider that departure from life is an unimportant matter even for a stranger, not to mention for our close friends, when they cease from living? We see," I said, "that

1 Basil the Great, Archbishop of Caesarea in Cappadocia, brother of Macrina and Gregory of Nyssa, died 1 January 379.
2 1 Thessalonians 4:13.

all human exertion is directed toward this one purpose, that we may remain in life. This is why we have invented houses for habitation, so that our bodies may not be overcome by their environment through cold or heat. What else is agriculture but a provision for living? Our concern for life undoubtedly arises from the fear of death. What about the practice of medicine? Why is it honored among men? Isn't it because it seems somehow by its arts to fight against death? Breastplates, shields, greaves, helmets, defensive weapons, circuit walls, iron gates, fortification ditches, and all this kind of thing—why else are they made, except because of the fear of death? So if death is naturally so fearsome, how can we easily obey when we are told that the survivor should refrain from grief for the dying?"

"What aspect of death seems to you most grievous in itself?" asked my teacher. "The habits of ignorant people are not sufficient reason for your aversion."

"What indeed! Isn't it worth grieving," I said to her, "when we see someone who was just now living and speaking, but all at once loses breath, voice, and movement, with all his natural faculties of perception quenched, with no ability to see or hear, or to use any other of the means by which perception receives its impressions? Even if you touch him with fire or steel, if you cut up his body with a sword, if you expose him to carnivorous beasts, if you bury him in the ground, none of these affects him at all. The principle of life (whatever it is) all at once becomes invisible and unseen, like a lamp that is put out when the flame which burned in it no longer remains even on the wick. It does not go to any other place, but altogether disappears. So when we see such changes, how could we endure them without grief, since we have nothing visible to rely on? When we hear that the soul has departed, we see what is left behind, but we do not know what is separated. We do not know what it is by nature nor where it has gone. Neither earth nor air nor water nor any other of the elements[3] reveals in itself the power which has

3   The theory that everything consists of four elements, fire, air,

gone out of the body. When that power has departed, what remains is a corpse and is already subject to corruption."

As I was saying this, my teacher interrupted me with a motion of her hand. "You are not disturbed, are you, or troubled in your mind, by a fear that the soul may not remain forever, but may cease from existence when the body disintegrates?"

I answered rather boldly, as my ability to reason had not yet entirely recovered from the experience of grief. I said, "The divine words are like commands, by which we are required to believe that the soul must remain forever. We have not been led to such a doctrine by any logical reasoning. It seems to me that our intellect accepts these orders by a kind of interior slavery, rather than assenting to the argument by a voluntary impulse. Because of this our grief over those who depart is the more painful, since we do not understand clearly whether that life-giving principle still exists in itself, or where and how it exists, or whether it no longer exists anywhere in any manner. Uncertainty about the truth gives equal weight to both assumptions. Many people hold one opinion, and many hold the opposite. There are also some among the pagans with a considerable reputation for philosophy who have held and taught these ideas."

"Forget," she said, "the futile talk of unbelievers, in which the inventor of falsehood persuasively concocts deceptive theories. As for you, consider this: such an attitude towards the soul would imply that you are hostile to virtue and care only for immediate pleasure. It would abolish all hope of eternal life, that hope which alone gives virtue an advantage."

"And how," I said, "can we gain a solid and stable belief concerning the permanence of the soul? I myself perceive that the life of men is deprived of that which is most beautiful in it (I mean

water, and earth, is attributed to Empedocles of Acragas, early
fifth century B.C. Here Macrina speaks loosely as if there were
an indefinite number of elements.

virtue), unless we possess an unambiguous faith on this point. For how can virtue have a place with those who suppose that the present life is the limit of their existence, and who hope for nothing more after this life?"

"That is why we must try to learn," said my teacher, "where our discussion may find the proper starting point for these questions. If you agree, let your part be to support the opposing doctrines, for I see that your inclination is stirred up to assume this role. In this way we will discover the truth, after we have presented the conflicting arguments."

When she directed me to do this, I entreated her not to think that I was contradicting her in seriousness, but only in order to establish securely the doctrine of the soul by demolishing the obstacles to this goal. "Surely," I said, "those who support the opposing argument would say that the body, being composite, must be dissolved into those elements from which it is composed. When the combination of the elements in the body is broken up, each element is likely to be drawn to its own kind. The very nature of the elements returns each to its own kind by some inevitable attraction.[4] The warmth in us is united to warmth, the earthy is united to the solid earth, and each of the other parts rejoins that which is related to it. So where will the soul be after this? Anyone who says that it is in the elements will have to admit that it is identical with them, for there could not be a mixture of unlike with unlike. If this happened, the soul would obviously be revealed as a complex thing, a combination of opposing qualities. That which is complex is not simple but must be composite. Every composite thing can necessarily be dissolved into its parts.[5] Dissolution is

4   The attraction of like to like was an axiom of early Greek science, assumed (for example) by Empedocles of Acragas and Anaxagoras of Clazomenae.
5   If a composite thing is resolved into its parts, we say that it is destroyed, even though the parts are not reduced to nothing-

effectively destruction for something which consists of parts. Whatever is destroyed is not immortal; otherwise the flesh also would be called immortal even though it is dissolved into the elements of which it consists. But if the soul is something else and in some other place than this, where does the argument suppose that it is? It cannot be in the elements if its nature is different, and there is no other place in the universe where the soul could be, if it is living in accordance with its own nature. Whatever is nowhere undoubtedly does not exist."

My teacher groaned softly at my words, and said, "The Stoics and Epicureans might have brought forward these words, and others like them, when they met the apostle Paul in Athens.[6] For indeed I hear that Epicurus especially was led in this direction by his assumptions. He conceived the nature of beings to be fortuitous and automatic because he believed that there was no providence pervading events. In consequence, therefore, he thought that human life also was like a bubble, inflated by some kind of breath from our body, as long as the breath is held in by its container; but when the swollen bubble bursts, then the contents are extinguished along with it. For him appearance was what defined the nature of beings, and he made perception the standard by which all things are comprehended. He completely closed the eyes of his soul and was unable to look at any of the bodiless things which are known by the intellect, just as someone who is shut up in a little hut remains unaware of the heavenly marvels because he is prevented by the walls and roof from seeing what is outside. All perceptible things which are seen in the universe are simply a sort of earthly walls which shut off small-souled people

ness. Plato's argument for the immortality of the soul requires that it be a simple entity which cannot be dissolved (see *Phaedo* 78C, *Republic* 611B).

6   Acts 17:18. What Macrina says here applies to the Epicureans, but not to the Stoics, who regarded the soul as material like the body. Macrina avoids seeming to be too well informed on pagan philosophy.

from the vision of intelligible things. Such a man looks only at earth, water, air, and fire. Where each of these comes from, or what it is in, or what it is contained by, he cannot see, because of the smallness of his soul. Anyone who sees a garment infers the weaver; from a ship one understands that there is a shipwright; the hand of a carpenter comes to the mind of the viewer along with the sight of a house; but those who look at the cosmos are dim-sighted with regard to the One who is revealed through it. For this reason these 'wise' and 'perceptive' assertions are presented by those who teach the annihilation of the soul: they say that the body comes from the elements and the elements from the body, and that the soul cannot exist by itself, if it is neither part of these bodily elements nor in them. If our opponents suppose that the soul is not anywhere because it does not have the same nature as the elements, first let them teach that bodily life is soulless (for the body is nothing other than a concurrence of the elements). They should not even say that the soul is in these elements, giving life by itself to their combination, if (as they suppose) it is not possible hereafter for the soul as well as the elements to continue in existence. By their arguments they would prove that our life is nothing but death. But if they do not doubt that the soul is in the body, how can they teach that it is destroyed when the body is resolved into its elements? Let them dare to say the same about the divine Nature itself! How will they say that the intellectual, immaterial, and invisible Nature puts on moisture and softness, warmth and solidity, and holds in existence the things that are, although it is not related to the things in which it occurs yet is not prevented by its unrelatedness from being in them? Therefore they must remove entirely from their teaching that very Divinity which maintains the universe."

"How could this point be doubtful to our opponents," I said, "that everything comes from God, and that in Him are maintained the things that exist? How can they doubt even that there exists something divine which surpasses the nature of all beings?"

She said, "It would be more fitting to keep silent concerning these matters, and not to consider the foolish and impious propositions worthy of an answer, especially since one of the divine sayings forbids us to answer the fool according to his folly.[7] He is undoubtedly a fool who, in the words of the prophet, says that there is no God.[8] But since it is necessary to speak about this also, I will tell you," she said, "a word, not indeed my own,[9] nor from any other human being (for we are small, however great we may be); but that which the creation of the universe narrates through the wonders which are in it, which the eye hears when the wise and artful word sounds in the heart through what is seen. Creation openly proclaims its Maker; the very heavens, as the prophet says, are telling the glory of God with silent voices.[10] We see the harmony of the universe, of the heavens and the terrestrial marvels. We see how elements which are opposed to one another by nature are all woven together towards the same purpose by some inexplicable association, each one contributing its own power for the permanence of the whole. Things which cannot be mixed or joined together according to their proper qualities nevertheless do not separate from one another, nor are they destroyed in one another by a confusion of their opposite qualities. Those whose nature tends upward are carried downward, as the warmth of the sun streams down in its rays. Heavy bodies are lightened and rarified in vapors, as when water contrary to its own nature moves upward, carried through the air by winds. The ethereal fire comes down to earth, so that the low places are not lacking in warmth. The moisture of rain poured out on the earth, although it is one in nature, begets a multitude of different plants, producing appropri-

7   Proverbs 26:4-5.
8   Psalm 13(14):1.
9   Allusion to the phrase from Euripides' lost play *Melanippe* quoted by Plato (*Symposium* 177A): "Not mine is the word which I am about to speak."
10 Psalm 18(19):1-4.

ate growth in all that exists. The swift revolution of the celestial sphere, the reverse movement of the inner orbits,[11] the occultations and conjunctions, and the harmonious oppositions of the stars: when we see all these with the intellectual eye of the soul, are we not taught plainly from our observations that a divine Power, appearing skillful and wise in the universe and permeating everything, fits the parts together with the whole and fulfills the whole in the parts? It maintains everything by one power, remaining in Itself and revolving around Itself. It never ceases its motion nor migrates into another place than that in which It is."

"And how," I said, "can a faith in the existence of God prove also that the human soul exists? The soul is not the same as God, so that, if we were to admit that the one exists, we would have to admit that the other exists as well."

She replied, "It is said by the wise that the human being is a kind of small cosmos, containing in himself the same elements with which the whole is built up.[12] If this is true (and it seems likely), perhaps we would not need any other assistance to confirm for us what we have assumed concerning the soul. We have assumed that it exists in itself, with its own nature, utterly different from the solidity of the body. As we observe the whole universe through sensual apprehension, by the very operation of our senses we are led to conceive of that reality and intelligence which surpasses the senses.[13] Our eyes become interpreters of the omnipotent wisdom which is contemplated in the universe, the wisdom which reveals through itself the One who maintains the whole in accordance with it. In the same way, when we look at the cosmos in ourselves, we

11 The planets appear to move back and forth in the sky relative to the fixed stars. The geocentric astronomical theory of Ptolemy accounts for these motions by a system of "epicycles."
12 Various Greek thinkers, perhaps beginning with Anaximenes of Miletus (sixth century B.C.), drew an analogy between man as the microcosm and the universe as the macrocosm.
13 Compare Wisdom 13:5.

have found a good place to start conjecturing about what is hidden from what appears. By 'hidden' I mean that which escapes the observation of the senses because in itself it can be known only by the intellect and not by sight."

CHAPTER 2

The Nature of the Soul

And I said, "Indeed we can make inferences about the wisdom which presides over the whole through the wise and skillful patterns in the harmonious order of this universe; but what knowledge of the soul could those who track down hidden truths obtain from what the body reveals?"

"Don't you see," the maiden said, "if we desire to know ourselves, in obedience to that wise precept,[1] the soul itself teaches us well enough what we should understand about the soul, namely that it is immaterial and bodiless, working and moving in accord with its own nature, and revealing its motions by means of the bodily organs. For the same arrangement of the bodily organs exists in the corpses of the dead, but the soul remains immobile and not activated by the psychic power which is no longer in it. It is moved when perception resides in the organs and intellectual power pervades perception, moving the organs of perception along with its own impulses as it chooses."

"What," I said, "is the soul, if its nature can be described in some definition, so that we may gain some understanding of the subject through the description?"

My teacher said, "Different authors have offered different descriptions of the soul, each defining it as he chooses, but my opinion concerning it is this: the soul is an essence which has a beginning; it is a living and intellectual essence which by itself gives to the organic and sensory body the power of life and

1 The famous maxim from the shrine of Apollo at Delphi, "Know thyself."

reception of sense-impressions as long as the nature which can receive these maintains its existence."

As she said this, she indicated with her hand the doctor who was sitting beside her to care for her body, and said, "The evidence for what I have said is close at hand. How does this man by laying his fingers on my artery hear somehow through the sense of touch how my nature calls out to him and explains its own condition? Because the sickness of my body is increasing; the disease arises from these internal organs, and the increase of the inflammation extends this far. His eye teaches him other things of this kind, as he looks at the way I am lying and how my flesh is wasting away. He sees how my interior condition is shown by the appearance of my complexion, pale and bilious, and the glance of my eyes, turning automatically towards the location of the pain. His hearing also gives him similar information, as he recognizes my trouble by the frequency of my breathing and the groan emitted along with my respiration. One could say that even the doctor's sense of smell informs him about my condition, because it recognizes by some particular quality of the breath the illness hidden in the internal organs. Could this be, if there were not some intelligent power present in each of the sensory organs? What would the hand by itself have taught us, if the mind did not lead the sense of touch to knowledge of the subject? What would the hearing apart from the mind, or the eye, or the nostril, or any other sense-organ, have contributed to the knowledge of the problem, if each of these existed by itself alone? But we remember the true saying of a man educated in pagan wisdom, that it is the mind which sees and the mind which hears.[2]

"If you do not admit that this is true, tell me, how is it that, when you look at the sun as you were taught by your teacher to look, you do not say that it is only as large as the circle which appears to

2   Epicharmus, fragment 249, quoted by Theodoret in *De Fide* I:
    "The mind sees and the mind hears; the rest is deaf and blind."

the average person, but that it exceeds by many times the size of the whole earth? Isn't it because when your mind has distinguished through the observed phenomena the particular motion of the sun, the intervals of time and space, and the causes of eclipses, you can confidently declare that it is so? And when you watch the waning and waxing of the moon, you are taught something else by the shape in which the moon appears: namely that it is itself without light according to its own nature, and that it revolves in the closest orbit to earth, but shines from the rays of the sun. The same happens with mirrors which receive the sun on themselves and send back rays which are not their own but come from the light of the sun, reflected back from the smooth and shiny body. To those who watch without examining the matter, however, that light seems to be from the moon itself. Here is the proof that it is not so. When the moon comes diametrically opposite the sun, it is illuminated on the whole circle facing toward us. In its own smaller space, however, as the moon goes more quickly around its circle, before the sun revolves once in its proper course, the moon goes around its own orbit more than twelve times.[3] Therefore the result is that the moon is not always filled with light; for in the frequency of its revolution the body which runs often around its short course does not remain continuously opposite the other body which travels farther around its longer orbit. When the moon is in a position directly opposite the sun, the whole side of the moon toward us is illuminated with the rays of the sun. When it comes sideways to the sun, as the hemisphere of the moon which at any time faces the sun is enveloped by its rays, the side towards us is necessarily shadowed. The brilliance changes places from the part which is not able to look towards the sun to that which is at any time turned towards it, until going directly under the orbit of the

3   If all motion is relative (as modern physics tells us), we can think of the earth as the center; the moon will revolve around the earth in a (lunar) month, and the sun in a year.

sun the moon receives its rays from behind. Thus when the upper
hemisphere is illuminated it makes the side towards us invisible
because it is entirely without light and radiance according to its own
nature. This is called the 'new moon.' But if again it goes past the
sun according to the proper motion of its course, and comes sideways to the rays, that which was just now without light begins to
shine a little, as the rays go around from that which was illuminated
to that which was previously dark. Do you see what your sight
teaches you? It would not provide you with such understanding by
its own power, if there were not something looking through the
sense of sight which can use the things which come to perception
as guides to penetrate through the appearances to that which does
not appear. Why should I mention the geometrical demonstrations
which lead us by visible figures to the knowledge of the invisible,
or innumerable other instances besides these, which show us that
we come to comprehend the intelligible essence which is hidden in
our nature through the functions which operate in our bodies?"

"But what about this possibility?" I said. "Materiality is common to the perceptible nature of the elements. Yet there are great
differences according to the peculiarities in each kind of matter, for
they have opposite motions, as one tends to move upward, while the
other sinks downward. They are not of the same kind and their
quality differs. One might say, according to the same argument, that
these elements have some power joined essentially with them
which effects these appearances of intelligence and these motions
out of their natural property and power. We see many such things
contrived by the makers of machines, in which they arrange matter
skillfully to imitate nature. Their contrivances do not show similarity to nature in appearance alone, but also sometimes in motion, and
in representation of a kind of voice, when the mechanism reverber-
ates in its sounding part. In such cases indeed the phenomenon does
not lead us to suppose that an intelligent power brings about in each
machine the appearance, form, sound, or motion. If we should say

that the same also happens in the case of this mechanical instrument of our nature, we might say that no intelligent essence is infused in us according to the peculiarity of our nature, but some kinetic power resides in the nature of the elements in us. Such activity would be a result. It would be nothing else but a certain impulsive motion which works toward the knowledge of that which we are eagerly studying. Which conclusion would be better supported by these arguments, that the intellectual and incorporeal essence of the soul exists by itself, or that it does not exist at all?"

"Our discussion," she said, "is assisted by your example, and the whole construction of the opposing argument will make no small contribution towards confirming what we have understood."

"What do you mean?"

"The very fact," she said, "of knowing how to handle and arrange the inanimate matter, so that the skill applied to the mechanisms all but serves instead of a soul for the material object (through these mechanisms the object imitates motion and sound, various shapes, and the like), would be proof that there is something in man of the sort that through imaginative and inventive power is able to understand machines within itself and to plan them in thought, and then to put them into action by skill and to manifest the thought in matter. For first a man recognized that moving air is required for the production of sound. Then he investigated by reasoning how air might be made to move in the machine. He considered the nature of the elements, knowing that no existing thing is empty. That which is light is called 'empty' by comparison with that which is heavier, since even air in itself according to its own substance is compact and full. A vessel is colloquially called 'empty' when it is empty of liquid, but all the same the educated person calls it full: full, that is, of air. The evidence is that the jar which is brought to the pond does not immediately fill with water. It floats on the surface at first, because the trapped air holds its belly upwards, until the jar pressed down by the hand of the water-drawer goes deeper in, and then receives the water in its mouth. This shows that the jar is not empty even before it is filled with the water. For a conflict of the two elements takes place at the mouth: the water is forced by its weight to flow into the belly; and the air which is trapped in the belly is compressed through the same mouth in the opposite direction to flow upwards past the water. The flow of air is interrupted by the water, and the water is made to gurgle and foam by the force of the moving air. The inventor observed this phenomenon and contrived through the nature of the elements a means to make air move in a machine. He built a kind of container from water-tight material, and enclosed the air in it with no leaks anywhere. Then he brought the water through a mouth to the inner cavity, measuring the amount of water necessary. Next he gave a passage to the air on the opposite side into the adjacent pipe. The air compressed more forcibly by the water began to move, and encountering the construction of the pipe, it made a sound.[4]

"Is it not clearly proved by what we can see that there is in man a mind, something else besides what we can see? By the invisible intelligence of its own nature the mind makes such plans by thought within itself; then, as we have described, through material assistance it brings into the open the concept which exists within. For if we should ascribe (as our opponents argue) such marvelous creations to the nature of the elements, we should undoubtedly see machines arising automatically. Bronze would not await art to take on human form, but would acquire this form immediately by its own nature. Air would not need a pipe to make a sound, but would

4   Macrina is referring to the "water-organ" (*hydraulis*) invented by Ctesibius of Alexandria (third c. B.C. pioneer in the use of air pressure). Apparently the water served to maintain the pressure of the air flowing from the inner cavity into the organ pipes, as the piper's elbow does for the air in bagpipes.

always resonate by itself, however it happens to flow and move. Water would not be forced to move upward through a channel, as now the inventor's art compels it by pressure to move contrary to its nature; it would surely go automatically towards the machine, carried upward by its own nature. In fact, however, none of these things is brought about automatically by the nature of the elements, but rather each is induced by art to accomplish the inventor's intention. Art is a kind of steadfast thought operating through matter towards some purpose, and thought is a kind of motion and operation proper to the mind. So even through the objections which you have adduced, the consequence of our reasoning has proved that the mind is something else besides that which we can see."

I said, "I myself admit that this is so. What is not visible differs from what is visible. Nevertheless I do not see the answer which we were seeking in this argument. For it is not yet clear to me what in the world we should consider that invisible thing to be. I have learned from your reasoning that it is not something material, but I do not yet know what we ought to say concerning it. What I especially wanted to learn is this: not what it is *not*, but what it *is*."

She said, "We learn a lot about many things, when we say that something is not such-and-such. By this method we can explain what the very being is of the thing we are seeking. We present the good by saying that it is not evil. We make cowardice known by naming it 'unmanliness.' We could mention many similar cases, in which either we understand the better concept through denial of the worse, or else we turn our thought in the other direction (from the better to the worse), displaying evil by the deprivation of good qualities. So, you see, if you will think about the implications of the present discussion as well, you will not miss the correct idea concerning the inquiry. For we are asking what we should think that the mind is according to its very essence. Let us suppose that you do not doubt that this thing exists which we are discussing, because you are convinced by its activity which we have demonstrated, but you want to know what it is. You would find out enough by learning that it is not anything which is comprehended by perception, neither color, nor shape, nor hardness, nor weight, nor size, nor tridimensionality, nor location in a place, nor any at all of the properties which we understand in reference to matter—if indeed it is something else besides these properties."

As she was expounding this, I said, "I do not know how it is possible, if all these things are removed from the discussion, to keep from eliminating the subject of the inquiry along with them. I do not see where the desire to understand may be attached apart from these. For wherever we investigate the things that exist through our examining thought, groping for the subject of the inquiry like blind men being led along the walls to the door, we must touch one of the things mentioned, finding either color, or shape, or size, or some other of the properties which you just now enumerated. But when we are told that the subject is none of these, we are led by the limitations of our soul to suppose that it is not anything at all."

"What foolishness!" she said. "How far will this petty and ignoble judgment go concerning the things which exist? If anyone denies existence to everything which is not known by sense-perception, he would have to deny also that very Power which oversees all and controls all that exists! When he learns that the divine nature is bodiless and invisible, by the same logic he will reason that it does not exist at all. But if, in the case of the divine, the lack of these qualities does not prove non-existence, how is the human mind eliminated from existence, as if it were completely consumed when the bodily properties are taken away?"

"And so in consequence of this," I said, "from one absurdity we deduce another absurdity. For our discussion leads us to conclude that our mind is the same as the divine nature, if we know each by removing that which is found by sense-perception."

"Don't say 'same,'" my teacher said. "This is another impious argument. Say, as you were taught by the inspired voice, that the one is *like* the other.[5] That which is made in the image of something else must keep in every respect a similarity to its archetype. The likeness of the intellectual is intellectual. The likeness of the bodiless is bodiless, freed from all weight and escaping all dimensional measurement like its archetype, but different from it according to the particular property of its nature. For it would not be an image if it were the same as its original in all respects. But whatever appears in the uncreated nature, the same appears in the created nature. Often in a small fragment of glass, when it happens to lie in the sunlight, the whole circle of the sun is seen, not appearing in it according to its own size, but as the smallness of the fragment allows the reflection of the sun's circle. In the same way the smallness of our nature reflects the images of those ineffable properties of divinity, so that our reasoning guided by these properties does not fail to comprehend the essence of the mind, because it dismisses the property of corporeality from its examination of the subject. Still we do not consider the small and perishable nature equal to the invisible and immortal. We suppose that its essence is intelligible, since it is an image of an intelligible essence, yet we do not say that the image is the same as the archetype.

"Because of the ineffable wisdom of God which appears in the universe, we are confident that the divine nature and power is in everything that exists, so that everything remains in existence. Of course, if one should ask about the principle of the nature, the essence of God is far distant from that which is revealed and understood in each created thing; yet we affirm that that which is different in nature is nevertheless found in these created things. In the same way, it is not at all incredible that the nature of the soul which is something else in itself (whatever it is thought to be) can exist, even though those things which appear as elements in the

5   Genesis 1:26-27.

cosmos differ from it in the principle of their nature. After all, even in living bodies (as we have said already[6]) which subsist from a mixture of the elements, the simplicity and invisibility of the soul and the solidity of the body have nothing in common according to the principle of their natures. Even so we do not doubt that the life-giving energy of the soul is in these bodies, combined with them in some manner beyond human comprehension.

"Therefore even when the elements in the body are resolved into themselves, the bond is not destroyed which united them through the activity of life. While the compound of the elements still holds together, each element receives life, because the soul enters equally and similarly into all the members which constitute the body. We could not say that that which is in all the elements of the body and inserts the power of life into each of them is solid and hard because it is mixed with the earthy element, nor could we say that it is moist and cold or has the opposite quality to coldness. Consequently also when the compound is dissolved and has returned again to its proper elements, it is quite plausible to suppose that the simple and uncompounded nature remains with each of the members even after the dissolution. That which has once been united in some ineffable manner to the compound of the elements would also remain forever with those elements with which it was mixed, without being in any way separated from the union which happened to it once and for all. When the composite part is dissolved, the uncompounded part is not likely to be dissolved also along with the composite part."

Then I said, "But no one would deny that the elements come together with each other and separate from each other, and that this is the creation and dissolution of the body. Since we recognize, however, that there is a great diversity among the heterogeneous elements, which differ from each other in local position and in the different properties of their qualities, when the elements come together

6   See above p. 32.

in the subject, this intelligent and dimensionless nature which we call 'soul' accordingly coalesces with their union. But if these elements are separated from each other and depart each to that place where its nature leads it, what will happen to the soul, when its vehicle is scattered in many directions? Just as a sailor, when his vessel is broken up in a shipwreck, cannot float on all the parts of the boat which have been scattered in different directions on the sea: surely he will take hold of whatever part he finds and let the waves carry away the rest; in the same manner, since the soul is naturally unable to be split up along with the separation of the elements, if indeed it is firmly attached to the body, it will surely join itself to some one of the elements and be divided from the others. The consequence of the reasoning does not allow us to suppose any more that the soul is immortal, because it lives in one element, than that it is mortal, because it is not in many of the other elements."

"But that which is intelligible and without dimension is neither contracted nor dispersed," she said. "Contraction and dispersal are proper to bodies. The soul, however, is equally present according to its own invisible and incorporeal nature at the aggregation of the elements into the body and at their segregation. It is not crowded when the elements are compressed in the aggregation, nor is it left behind when they return to what is related and connatural to them, even though there seems to be a great diversity which appears in the variety of the elements. For the difference is great between that which is light and upward-moving and that which is heavy and earth-bound, and between the warm and the cold, and the moist and its opposite. Nevertheless it is no trouble for the intellectual nature to be present with each of the elements to which it was once joined in their mixture, without being split up by the incompatibility of the elements. For although the elements seem distant from each other according to their local position and proper quality, this does not trouble the dimension-less nature which is attached to elements locally separated, since even now it is possible for the mind at the same time to contemplate heaven and to stretch to the limits of the universe in its curiosity,[7] and the contemplative faculty of our soul is not torn apart as it stretches for such a distance. Therefore nothing hinders the soul from being present to the elements of the body both when they are mixed together by their combination and when they are dissolved by their separation. When gold and silver are welded together a certain artistic power is envisioned which fuses the materials together; and if again the one is melted away from the other, none the less the principle of the art remains in each. The material is separated into parts, but the art is not split along with the material. For how could the indivisible be divided? According to the same reasoning the intellectual nature of the soul appears in the combination of the elements and does not disappear when they are dissolved, but it remains in them. Although it is stretched out with their separation it is not cut apart, nor is it chopped into parts and pieces according to the number of the elements. For division is proper to the bodily and dimensional nature, but the intellectual and dimensionless nature does not suffer the accidents which happen because of dimension. Therefore the soul is in those elements which it has once entered, and no necessity breaks it off from its union with them. So what cause for sadness is there in this, if the invisible is received in exchange for the visible? Why is your mind so filled with resentment towards death?"[8]

7   Compare Plato's *Theaetetus* 173E: "...[the philosopher's] thought...takes wings...searching the heavens and measuring the plains..."
8   Macrina refers back to the intial question, "Why do we fear death?" (above p. 28).

CHAPTER 3

The Emotions

I took up in my mind the definition which she had given in the earlier discussion concerning the soul, and said, "This discussion has not showed me clearly enough which powers are supposed to be in the soul. Your definition says that the soul is an intellectual essence which puts a living power into the organic body.[1] Our soul is not active only for the understanding and contemplative mind, accomplishing such operations in the intellectual faculty of its essence, nor does it manage only the organs of perception for their natural activity. The soul obviously has a great impulse of desire and another great impulse of anger. We see each of these impulses, which belong to us as human beings, producing many different results by their combined activity. We can observe many actions in which the desiring faculty takes the lead, and again many which arise because of anger. None of these comes from the body; but what is not bodily is undoubtedly intellectual. The definition has declared that the soul is some kind of intellectual thing, so one or the other of two absurdities emerges from the course of the reasoning. Either both anger and desire are other souls in us, and a multitude of souls appears instead of one; or else not even the faculty of thought may be considered a soul in us. For since intellect is attached equally to all these faculties, either it will prove that all of these are souls, or it will remove each of them equally from what is proper to the soul."

She said, "You have raised in your turn this question which has already been asked by many others, what we should consider

1 Above p. 37-38.

these faculties to be (the faculties of desire and anger), whether they are essentially joined to the soul and belong right from the beginning to its constitution, or whether they are something else besides the soul and are added to us later. Everyone agrees equally that these appear in the soul; but what we should think about them reason has not yet discovered with accuracy, so that we may have a notion concerning them which is trustworthy. Most people are still in doubt, holding unstable and diverse opinions concerning these faculties. For us, if the truth could be sufficiently demonstrated by the secular philosophy which has discoursed skillfully concerning these faculties, it would perhaps be superfluous to add a discussion of the soul to our investigation. But although some could theorize freely concerning the soul as the consequence of their reasoning led them, we have no part in this freedom (I mean the freedom to say whatever we want), since we always use the holy Scripture as the canon and rule of all our doctrine. So we must necessarily look towards this standard and accept only that which is congruent with the sense of the writings. Therefore we shall abandon the Platonic chariot and the pair of horses yoked to it, which pulled unequally, and the charioteer controlling these horses, through all of which Plato presents symbolically a philosophy concerning these faculties in relation to the soul.[2] We shall leave behind also whatever the philosopher who followed him set forth, he who skillfully observed the phenomena and examined carefully the subject which concerns us now, inferring that the soul is mortal.[3] We shall also set aside those who philosophized before these men and those afterwards, those who wrote in prose or in some rhythm and meter.[4]

2 *Phaedrus* 246A ff.
3 In *On the soul* 2.1 (413A3-5), Aristotle says that the soul is inseparable from the body. Later in the same treatise, however, he says that mind is immortal and eternal (3.6, 430A23).
4 Some of the "Presocratic" philosophers, such as Xenophanes of Colophon, Parmenides of Elea, and Empedocles of Acragas, expressed their ideas in verse.

"For our discussion we shall fix our eyes on the mark of the inspired Scripture, which establishes the law that we should consider nothing peculiar to the soul which is not also proper to the divine nature. For he who said that the soul is a likeness of God[5] has proclaimed that everything which is alien to God is outside the definition of the soul, for the likeness would not be preserved if there were differences. Therefore, since clearly no such thing as desire or anger appears in the divine nature,[6] logically one would suppose that these are not essentially united with the soul either. We shall decline to confirm our doctrine also by dialectical art through syllogistic and analytical methods, because such reasoning is unreliable and suspect for the demonstration of truth. Everyone knows that dialectical elaboration has equal power on both sides, to overturn the truth and to accuse falsehood. Hence we are often suspicious of the truth itself, if it is presented with this kind of art, as if such cleverness might mislead our mind and deceive it of the truth.[7] But if someone would accept an unadorned discourse, bare of all disguise, we will tell it, bringing out the theory concerning these faculties, as far as possible according to the sequence of the scriptural narrative.

"So what are we saying? Even those outside our system of thought testify that this rational animal, man, is capable of thought and understanding. Their definition would not describe our nature in this way if they supposed that anger and desire and everything of that sort were united essentially with our nature. One would not define any other subject by mentioning the common quality instead of the particular. So since the faculties of desire and anger appear

5   According to Genesis 1:27, man, not his soul only, is created in God's image.
6   A Platonist reading of the Old Testament apparently discounts the references to God's wrath and jealousy.
7   Macrina disparages logic, as if to avoid seeming too friendly to secular learning, while nevertheless using logic in her exposition.

equally in the irrational and the rational nature, one would not reasonably characterize the proper by the common. But if this faculty is rejected as superfluous for the description of our nature, how can it have the power to overthrow the definition, as if it were a part of the nature? For every definition of an essence looks toward the proper quality of the subject. That which is outside of the proper quality is omitted as alien to the definition. But the activity according to anger and desire is recognized to be common to all irrational nature. Whatever is common is not the same as that which particularizes. Consequently, we must not reckon these faculties among those by which the human nature is particularly characterized. If someone sees the perceiving, the nourishing, and the growing faculties in us, he does not reject because of these the given definition of the soul (for it is not the case that because one thing is in the soul, another is not); so also even though we have observed the impulses of the soul related to anger and desire, we could not reasonably oppose the definition on the grounds that it was deficient in representing the soul."

"So what should we learn about these faculties?" I asked my teacher. "If they are in us, I cannot yet see how we may set them aside as being alien to our nature."

"Do you see," she asked, "that reason conflicts with these faculties, and yearns for the soul to be stripped of them as far as possible? And indeed there are some for whom this yearning has been fulfilled, as we hear in the case of Moses, that he was superior to anger and desire.[8] The narrative testifies about him both that he was very meek, more than all men[9] (it shows his peaceableness and his freedom from anger by his meekness), and that he did not desire any of those things with which we see the desiring faculty concerned in most men. This would not have happened, if these faculties were part of our nature and were referred to the principle of our

8   What about, for example, Exodus 2:12 and 32:19?
9   Numbers 12:3.

essence, for it is not possible for one who has gone outside his nature to remain in being. But Moses was in being and yet was without these. Therefore these are something besides our nature, and not our nature itself, for the true nature is that which contains the being of the essence; but we can separate ourselves from these, in such a way that their disappearance is not only harmless but even beneficial to our nature. So obviously they are external, things which happen to our nature and do not belong to its essence. For the essence is what our nature is essentially.

"But many people think that anger is a seething of the blood around the heart; others, that it is an appetite for retaliating upon one who has troubled you.[10] But as I suppose, anger is an impulse to harm the one who provokes you. None of these fits in with the definition of the soul. And if we define desire in itself, we will say that it is a yearning for what we lack, or a longing for the enjoyment of pleasure, or a distress because what we want is not in our power, or an attachment to a pleasure which we may not enjoy. All of these, and others like them, illustrate desire, but do not touch the definition of the soul. Furthermore, whatever else appears around the soul, the qualities which appear in pairs of opposites, such as cowardice and boldness, misery and pleasure, fear and contempt, and the like, each of these seems indeed to be related to desire and anger, yet indicates its own nature by a particular definition. For boldness and contempt suggest a kind of manifestation of the angry impulse, while the attitude of cowardice and fear suggests a diminution and reduction of this same impulse. Misery, however, has material from both impulses: for anger which is too weak to take vengeance on those who have previously troubled us becomes misery, and despair and deprivation of the things which we desire also create this condition in the mind.

10 According to Aristotle (*On the soul* 1.1, 403A30-31), the former definition would be given by a natural scientist, the latter by a dialectician.

The condition which appears opposite to misery (I mean the sense of pleasure) likewise has a share in both anger and desire; for pleasure rules equally over both of these. All of these conditions are around the soul and are not the soul itself. They are like warts growing on the mental part of the soul which seem to be parts of it because they grow on it, but they are not what the soul is in its essence."[11]

"Nevertheless," I said to the maiden, "we see that virtuous people receive no little assistance towards the good from these faculties. For Daniel's desire was praiseworthy,[12] and Phineas placated God by his anger.[13] We have learned that the beginning of wisdom is fear,[14] and we have heard from Paul that the end of godly grief is salvation.[15] The Gospel prescribes for us contempt for terrible things,[16] and not to fear any fright is simply the description of boldness, which indeed was reckoned among good things by wisdom.[17] Therefore the divine word proves by these examples that we should not consider such emotions to be disorders, for disorders would not be employed to assist in the establishment of virtue."

My teacher said, "I myself was probably responsible for this confusion of reasoning, because I did not make distinctions in the discussion of this matter, which would give some logical order to our consideration. So now, as well as I can, I will devise an order for the investigation, so that as we consider the subject in logical order, we may leave no room for such objections. I say that the powers of contemplation, judgment, and vision of reality are proper and natural

11 In *Republic* X (611D), Plato compares the soul's evil accretions to barnacles and seaweed which disguise the form of the sea-god Glaucus.
12 Daniel 9:23; 10:11; 10:19; "man of desires" (variant reading in the Greek Bible).
13 Numbers 25:6-15.
14 Proverbs 1:7; 9:10.
15 2 Corinthians 7:10.
16 Luke 21:9 and parallels.
17 1 Peter 3:6.

to our soul, and that the soul keeps in itself through these powers the image of the divine Grace. Since also our reasoning conjectures that the divine, whatever it is in its own nature, is in these faculties at any rate, in the oversight of everything and the discrimination between the good and the worse. But whatever faculties lie on the boundary of the soul, inclining in opposite directions according to their own nature, which depending on their usage have a good or evil outcome, such as anger or fear or whatever of this kind is among the impulses of the soul, without which we cannot imagine human nature—we judge that these things have become attached to the soul from outside, because no such mark appears on the archetypal beauty. Only so far let our discussion concerning these be set forth as if in a lecture-hall, so that it may avoid the abuse of those who listen in order to criticize.

"The holy word tells how the Divine proceeded by a certain route and orderly sequence to the creation of mankind. For when the universe had taken shape, as the narrative says, man did not immediately come onto the earth, but the nature of irrational animals preceded him, and plants preceded the animals. By this, I suppose, the Scripture shows that the power of life mixes with the bodily nature in a certain sequence. First it enters those beings which lack sense-perception, but after them it proceeds to those with sense-perception; then in turn it ascends to the intelligent and rational creatures.[18] Therefore, of the beings which exist, some are corporeal and the rest are wholly intellectual. Of the corporeal, one part is inanimate, the other part animate (by animate, I mean partaking of life). Of living things, some are endowed with sense-perception, and the rest lack this faculty. Again, of those with sense-perception, some are rational, the rest irrational. Consequently, since the life of perception could not exist apart from

18 Although this discussion purports to be based on Genesis 1, the division of souls into vegetable, animal, and rational comes from Aristotle's treatise *On the soul*.

matter, nor could intellect enter into the body if it were not united with perception, for this reason the creation of mankind is narrated last. Humanity encompasses every form of life, including that which appears in the plants and that which appears in the irrational animals. From the vegetable form of life we have the capability of being nourished and growing; for this sort of activity can be seen in plants also, as they draw nourishment in through roots and send it forth into fruits and leaves. Moreover, from the irrational animals we have the capability of regulating our activity according to sense-perception. Thought and reason, however, are exclusive properties of our nature, as understood in themselves. Our nature has a power to take in the necessities for material life. As this power occurs in us it is called appetite. We say that this is from the vegetable form of life, since in plants also we can see certain impulses operating naturally when they are filled with what is proper to them and when they swell towards growth outwards. In the same way, whatever faculties are proper to the irrational nature are mixed with the intellectual power of our souls. From the animals," she said, "is anger, from them is fear, from them all the other qualities which conflict in us, except for the reasoning and thinking power, which indeed alone is distinctive of our nature, having (as we have said[19]), in itself the imitation of the divine character. Moreover, according to our previous reasoning, the rational power cannot enter into the bodily life otherwise than by entering through perception. Perception existed already in the nature of the irrational animals.

"Necessarily, therefore, through the faculty of perception our soul becomes associated also with the traits which are joined with perception. These are the traits which, when they occur in us, are called 'passions,' which were not bequeathed to human life solely for evil (for the Creator would bear the blame for evil, if because of them the necessity of transgression had been built into our nature).[20]

19 See above p. 54.
20 Notice that here the emotions, as well as other animal faculties,

Instead, by the particular use of our free choice such impulses of the soul become instruments of virtue or wickedness, just as steel, forged according to the intention of the craftsman, is shaped towards whatever the smith desires, becoming either a sword or some agricultural implement. Therefore if reason, which is the distinctive property of our nature, should gain dominion over those traits which are added to us from outside (the word of the Scripture has also revealed this as if in a riddle, bidding mankind to rule over all the irrational creatures[21]), none of these impulses would work in us for servitude to evil, but fear would produce obedience in us, anger courage, cowardice caution, and the desiring impulse would mediate to us the divine and immortal pleasure. But if reason should let go of the reins and like some charioteer entangled in the chariot should be dragged behind it,[22] wherever the irrational motion of the yoke-animals carries it, then the impulses are turned into passions, as indeed we can see also in the irrational animals. For when reason does not control the impulse which naturally lies in them, the fierce animals are destroyed by anger because they fight among themselves. The husky and powerful gain no benefit to themselves from the use of their strength, but become subject to the rational creatures because of their irrationality. In these animals the energy of desire and pleasure is not occupied with anything lofty, nor does any other of the faculties which appear in them lead in any way to a beneficial result. So also in us, if these faculties are not directed by reason

are attributed to man as created by God. This does not seem entirely consistent with what Macrina says later (below p. 114).

21 Genesis 1:28.
22 A charioteer wrapped the reins around his waist to keep his hands free for the whip, with the result that he risked being dragged by the chariot in the case of an accident. We are reminded again of the "Platonic chariot" (*Phaedrus* 246B), which Macrina earlier asked us to abandon.

towards what is right, but if instead the passions rule over the power of the mind, our humanity is changed from intelligence and god-likeness to irrationality and mindlessness. We are turned into beasts by the force of these passions."

I was very much impressed by what she had said. "For anyone who has sense," I replied, "your discussion, proceeding straightforwardly in order without adornment, is sufficient. It will appear to be correct and to contain the whole truth. But although a syllogism is enough to convince those who study technical methods of demonstration, we for our part agree that that which is revealed by the sacred doctrines of Scripture is more trustworthy than all the technical deductions. I think, therefore, that we should inquire whether the divinely inspired teaching agrees with what has been said."

She replied, "Who would deny that truth resides only in that upon which the scriptural testimony has set its seal? So if we need to employ also some evidence from the teaching of the Gospels for the defense of this doctrine, it would not be inappropriate for us to consider the parable of the tares.[23] In that story the householder planted good seed; we are undoubtedly his household. When the enemy had observed the men sleeping, he sowed the useless weeds among the nourishing crops, putting the tares in the midst of the grain. And the seeds sprouted alongside each other, for it was inevitable that the seed planted along with the grain would also sprout along with it. Because the useless plants were entangled with the roots of their opposite, the overseer of the farm prevented the servants from pulling them up, in order that the nourishing grain might not be pulled up along with the other kind. We suppose that the Scripture is representing those impulses of the soul by the healthful seeds. If only each of them had been cultivated for good, it would undoubtedly have produced the fruit of virtue for us. But since error in the judgment of the good[24] has been sown along with

23 Matthew 13:24-30.
24 Socrates taught that people always seek what they believe to

these impulses, that which alone is truly good by nature has also been overshadowed by the plant of deceit growing up along with it. For the desiring faculty has grown and matured not towards the good by nature, for the sake of which it was sown in us, but instead it has made the harvest beastly and irrational. This is where the impulse of desire has been led by misjudgment concerning the good. In the same way also the seed of anger has not been tempered into courage, but has armed us for battle with our own kind. Likewise the power of love has turned away from the intelligible, running riot in the immoderate enjoyment of the sensual. The other emotions in the same way have produced the worse plants instead of the better. For this reason the wise farmer allows the plant which has grown in with the seed to remain with it, taking care that we may not be deprived of the better part, as we might be if desire were altogether rooted out along with the useless growth. For if this should happen to our human nature, what is there which would raise us towards the union with the heavenly? Or if love[25] is taken away, in what manner will we be joined with the divine? If anger is quenched, what weapon will we have against our adversary? So you see the farmer leaves the bastard seeds in us, intending not that they should permanently dominate the more honorable sowing, but that the field itself (for so he figuratively names the heart) through the natural power residing in it (which is reason), should dry up one part of the plants, but render the other part fruitful and thriving. But if this does not happen, he assigns to the fire the task of sorting out the harvest.

"Therefore if a person uses these emotions according to the right principle, receiving them in himself without falling into their

be good, so if you know truly what is good you will necessarily act virtuously (see Plato's *Meno* 77C-E).

25 The word "love" (ἀγάπη) appears here, but we have not yet heard how it is related to "desire" (ἐπιθυμία).

power, he will be like some king who, by using the many hands of his servants for assistance, will easily accomplish his virtuous purpose. If, however, as when slaves revolt against their owner, he falls into the power of his emotions and is enslaved by them, succumbing ignobly to servile mindlessness, so that he becomes a puppet of those impulses which by nature are subjected to him, he will be drawn inevitably to those actions to which he is forced by the domination of the passions which control him. If this is true, we shall declare that these emotions are neither virtuous nor wicked in themselves, since they are impulses of the soul which lie in the power of the users to serve good or otherwise. When their movement is toward the better, we shall declare that they are material for praise, as desire was for Daniel, anger for Phineas, and grief for the one who mourns rightly. If, on the other hand, their inclination is towards the worse, then they become passions and are named accordingly."

CHAPTER 4

The Condition of the Soul after Death

After she had finished this exposition, when she ceased and made a short pause in her discourse, I recollected in my mind what she had said. Returning again to the earlier line of reasoning in which she had maintained that it is not impossible for the soul to be in the elements after the body has been dissolved,[1] I said this to my teacher: "Where does that notorious name of 'Hades' fit in? It is much used not only in the habitual speech of our daily life but also in the writings both of the pagan unbelievers and of our own Christian authors. Into it, everyone supposes, just as into some kind of receptacle, the souls pass over when they leave this life. For you would not call the elements 'Hades.'"

My teacher replied, "You obviously have not paid too much attention to the argument. When I said that the soul passes over from the visible to the invisible, I did not think that I had omitted anything in regard to the question of Hades. For it seems to me that when both the unbelievers and the holy Scripture use this name and say that the souls are 'in' it, they mean simply the transition to the invisible and unseen."[2]

"And how," I asked, "do some people suppose that the underground place is called by this name, and that it receives in itself the souls, as if it were a place which could receive their kind of nature, drawing to itself those which have already flown out of human life?"

---

1 Above pp. 46-48.
2 Plato etymologized "Hades" as from ἀειδῆ, "invisible" (*Phaedo* 80D).

"Our teaching will not be harmed by this opinion either," my teacher said. "For if what you say is true,[3] that the heavenly sphere is continuous with itself and uninterrupted, encompassing everything in its own circle, and that in the middle of it the earth and its surroundings are suspended, and that the motion of everything which revolves occurs around the axis which is fixed and stable, it must also be true," she said, "that whatever happens to each of the elements in the part above the earth, the same happens on the opposite side as well, since one and the same essence spreads all the way around the earth's whole mass. When the sun appears above the earth, its shadow is turned toward the part lying under the earth, as the earth's spherical shape is not able to be embraced at the same time all the way around by the covering of the sun's rays. Whatever part of the earth the sun strikes with its rays will undoubtedly be centered at some point on the sphere, and the other side diametrically opposite will inevitably be dark. And so the dark area moves continuously along with the sun's course opposite to the straight direction of the rays, so that the place above the earth and the place below the earth are equally by turns in light and in darkness. Thus we cannot reasonably doubt that all the other things which appear in elemental form in our hemisphere of the earth occur likewise around on the other side. Since the covering of the elements is one and the same over every part of the earth, I suppose that we need not either contradict or agree with those who claim that either this side or the subterranean place must be assigned to the souls which have been released from their bodies. As long as their objection does not disturb the principal doctrine concerning the existence of the souls after the life in the flesh, our discourse will not be at all troubled about the place. After all, we understand that location in a place is a property of bodies only, but that the soul, being bodiless, gets from its nature no need to be contained in particular places."

"What then," I said, "if the opponent should cite the apostle,

3   Macrina implies that she learned astronomy from Gregory.

who says that all the rational creation at the restoration of the universe looks toward the Governor of the whole? Among the rational creation he mentions certain subterranean beings, saying in the Epistle to the Philippians that to Him every knee shall bend of heavenly, earthly, and subterranean creatures." [4]

"We shall persist in our doctrine," said my teacher, "even if we hear them saying these things, since we have even our opponent in agreement with us concerning the existence of the soul; but we will not argue about the place, as I have said before."

"Then if we seek the apostle's meaning in this passage," I said, "what should we say, if we interpret the saying in reference to something other than a place?"

"It does not seem to me," she said, "that when the divine apostle distinguishes the intellectual essence by location, he means that one kind is something heavenly, a second kind something earthly, and a third kind something subterranean. But since the rational nature occurs in three states, the one being allotted the bodiless life from the beginning, which we name angelic, the second entwined with the flesh, which we call human, and the third released from the flesh by death, that which is understood to be in the souls,[5] I suppose that the apostle, seeing this in the depth of his wisdom, signifies the harmony of all the rational nature in the good which at some time will come into existence. He calls 'heavenly' the angelic and bodiless state, 'earthly' that which is involved in the body, and 'subterranean' that which is already separated from the body. Or if indeed any other nature besides those mentioned is imagined to exist among the rational beings, which one might wish to name either demons or spirits or any-

4   Philippians 2:10.
5   Macrina agrees with Origen (in his *On first principles*) that angels and human souls are of the same kind, but differs from him in supposing that the "subterranean" beings are human souls after death.

thing else of the sort, we will not differ, for it is believed both from the common notions and from the tradition of the Scriptures that there is some nature outside of bodies like ours, opposed to the good and harmful to human life, which has voluntarily fallen away from the better portion and in rebellion from the good gives substance to that which is conceived as its opposite. Some say that the apostle counts this demonic nature among the subterranean beings, signifying in that passage that when evil is finally obliterated by the long cycles of the ages, nothing outside of the good will remain, but the confession of Christ's lordship will be unanimous even from the demons.[6] Therefore no one could force us any longer by the name of subterranean beings to imagine a place under the earth, especially since we understand that the air is evenly wrapped around the earth everywhere, so that no part of the earth lacks the mantle of air."

6   This is the view of Origen, who suggested that all rational beings might eventually be redeemed.

CHAPTER 5

How Does the Soul Recognize the Elements of Its Body?

As my teacher expounded these matters, I hesitated a little before saying, "I do not yet have a sufficient hold of the subject. My mind is still somehow doubtful about what you have said. Would you please bring the discourse back again to the same line of reasoning, leaving out the matters on which we have already agreed? I suppose those who are not too contrarily disposed will be adequately persuaded neither to relegate the soul to destruction and non-existence after the dissolution of its body, nor to maintain that it cannot be anywhere among existing things because it is different in nature from the essence of the elements. Even if the intellectual and immaterial nature does not accord with the elements, it is not prevented from being in them.[1] This notion is confirmed for us in two ways: because now in this life the soul is in the body although it differs from the body in its essence; and because reason shows that the divine Nature, although it is wholly other than the perceptible and material essence, nevertheless pervades each of the things that exist and by its mixing with the universe holds the things which exist in being.[2] Following these analogies we suppose that the soul is not outside of the things which exist either, even when it migrates from the life which appears in a shape to that which is invisible. But how," I said, "since the united elements take up by their mixture with one another a different form, to which the soul has become accus-

1 See above p. 46.
2 See above pp. 33-34.

tomed, when at the dissolution of the elements the form is probably obliterated as well—what sign will the soul follow after this, when the familiar sign does not remain?"

After a little pause she said, "May I be granted the power to fashion some kind of analogy as an example to support our case, even if what I say seems outside possibility.[3] Let us imagine it to be possible for the painter's art, not only to mix the colors from opposites, as they are accustomed to do, for the likeness of a form, but also to separate what has been mixed, and to give back to each of the colors the hue which it has by nature. Suppose that white and black, or red and gold, or any other hue, are mixed together for the likeness of the subject, and again that the pigment should be separated from its mixture with the other and should return to itself. We would say that the very appearance of the color is still known by the artist. He would not at all forget either the red or the black, if, after being changed by their mixture with each other, they should again return to their natural hue. We would say that he remembers how the colors were combined with others. He knows what color he produced from the mixture of what pigments, and how when one color was washed out the other returned again to its own proper lustre. If he should need to mix the equivalent color again, the preparation will be less troublesome for him since he has practiced it in his preceding creative work. If indeed this analogy has some relevance for our discourse," she said, "we must examine the subject itself. Instead of the painter's art let the soul be the subject of our discourse, and instead of the colors of art let us consider the nature of the elements. The mixture of the variegated hue of the different colors, and likewise the hypothetical return of these to their own nature, will represent the conjunction and separation of the elements. We say in the example that the artist is not ignorant of the hue of the pigment when it returns again after its mixture to

3 Empedocles compared the combinations of the elements to the mixing of paints (fragment 23).

its own color, but knows both the red and the black and whatever else has produced the form through a sort of communion with something heterogeneous. He knows them as they were in the mixture of colors and as they are now when they have gone back to their nature, and as they will be again, if the colors should be mixed again with one another in like manner. In the same way we say that, even after their dissolution, the soul knows the individual nature of the elements which joined together in the formation of the body to which it was attached. Even if their nature drives them far away from one another because of their inherent oppositions, repelling each of them from the combination with its opposite, none the less the soul will be present with each, holding on to its own by its cognitive power and remaining with it until the separated elements are combined again into the same body to reconstitute what was dissolved. This in a true sense both is and may properly be called 'resurrection.'"

And I said, "You seem to me in passing to have excellently defended the principle of the resurrection. You might be able to dissuade gently by this reasoning those who oppose the faith from supposing that it is impossible for the elements to come together again with one another and to reproduce the same man."

"Yes," said my teacher, "what you say is true; for we may hear those who object to this principle saying, 'When the elements have been resolved into the universe and rejoined their own kind, how can that which is warm in this life, after it has returned to its pure state in the universe, again be separated from its own kind in order to constitute the man who is to be formed again? For if it should not recover its own exactly, but should use some material of the same kind instead of its very own, it will become a different one in place of the one it was before. Such an event would no longer be resurrection but the fashioning of a new man. But if the same man must return to himself again, he ought to be altogether the same as himself, taking up again his original nature in all the parts of the elements.'"

"Therefore," I said, "against this objection also, it would be sufficient for us to maintain this conception concerning the soul, that whatever elements were joined to the soul at the beginning, it remains with them even after their dissolution, stationed like a guard over its own. When the elements mix with their own kind, the soul does not let go of its own in the subtlety and mobility of its intellectual power. It is not deceived by the small particles of the elements, but it slips away together with its own when they are mixed with their kind. It does not become weak as it passes through small spaces with them, when they are poured out into the universe, but it always remains in them, wherever and however their nature arranges them. If various strands of rope are fastened to one starting point, all of them together will follow at the same time when one is pulled. In the same way, if the Power which governs the universe should send to the dissolved elements the signal for coming together, then by one power of the soul the diverse elements will be drawn together. In the concurrence of its own elements the rope of our body will be braided by the soul. Each element in order will be woven again to its former accustomed place and will wrap around that which is familiar to it."

"Here is another analogy," said my teacher, "which we may reasonably add to those which we have examined before, to prove that it is not very difficult for the soul to distinguish its own elements from those which do not belong to it. Suppose that some clay is set before a potter. Imagine that there is a lot of clay, of which some is already formed for the fabrication of some kind of vessel, but the rest is waiting to be formed later. Let not all the vessels be of the same shape, but one a big storage-jar, one a wine-pitcher, another a plate or bowl or some other of the items necessary for daily use. Let these belong not all to one man, but, for the sake of argument, let each have its own master. As long as each of these vessels is in one piece, they are recognized by their owners. If they are smashed, none the less the possessors can tell even from the fragments what is from the storage-jar and what piece is from the drinking-cup. If the pieces should be mixed into the unworked clay, the fragments which have previously been worked can be distinguished from it even more surely. Similarly, each man is a kind of vessel, formed from a common material by the conjunction of elements, which undoubtedly has in its particular form much difference from the others of its kind. When the vessel is dissolved, the soul which has possessed it continues to recognize its own vessel just as well from the mere remains. The soul does not depart from its own elements either when the fragments are collected together or if they are mixed with the unworked part of the elemental matter. The soul always knows its own body as it is when it coheres in its shape; and it is not deceived concerning its own body after the dissolution, because of the signs which persist in the remnants."

I accepted that her illustrations were suitable and appropriate for the purpose which we had set ourselves. "It is good," I said, "to say and believe these things. But if someone should cite in objection to our words the narrative in the Gospel of the Lord concerning those in Hades,[4] alleging that it is not in accord with our findings, how should we prepare to answer him?"

She said, "Although that parable presents the narrative in rather corporeal terms, yet it scatters many clues which challenge us, if we listen attentively, to a more subtle interpretation. When the Lord separates evil from good by a great gulf, when He makes the anguished man need a drop of water brought by a finger and offers the bosom of the patriarch as a resting-place for the one who suffers evil in this life, and before all these tells how both men were dead and buried, He leads us far beyond the ordinary understanding if we follow with intelligence what He says. For what kind of eyes does the rich man lift up in Hades, when he has left

4   The parable of the rich man and Lazarus, Luke 16:19-31.

the eyes of the flesh in the tomb? How does his bodiless soul feel
the fire? What kind of tongue does he desire to have cooled with a
drop of water, when he no longer has his fleshly tongue? What is
the finger which brings the drop to him? The bosom of rest itself,
what is it? For when the bodies are in the tombs, and the soul neither
remains in the body nor consists of parts, we could hardly reconcile
the narrative with the truth if we should keep to the ordinary
understanding. We would have to transfer each item to intellectual
contemplation, so as to consider (for example) that the gulf is not a
gap in the earth, but rather the barrier which prevents incompatible
things from coming together. What trouble would it be for the
bodiless and intellectual soul to fly across a chasm, however great
it might be, since that which is intellectual by nature goes instanta-
neously wherever it wishes?"

"Then what would the fire be," I asked, "or the gulf, or the rest
of the things which have been mentioned, if they are not what their
names imply?"

"The Gospel seems to me," she said, "to signify by each of
these things certain doctrines relevant to our inquiry about the soul.
When the patriarch says at first to the rich man, 'You received your
share of good things by your life in the flesh,' and concerning the
beggar he says similarly, 'This man fulfilled his duty by his life of
partaking in evils,' he then goes on to mention the gulf by which
they are separated from each other. These words of his seem to
indicate a great doctrine here. In my opinion, the doctrine is this:
human life was originally uniform (by uniform I mean the life
which exhibits the good only, unmixed with evil). This opinion is
attested by God's first law, which gave to mankind unstinting
participation in every one of the good things of paradise, excluding
only that which had as its nature a mixture of opposites, evil
combined with good.[5] Death was set as a penalty for the violator of
this law. But man by the impulse of his free will voluntarily

5   Genesis 2:17.

abandoned the portion unmixed with evil and took for himself the life compounded from opposites. Nevertheless the divine Providence did not leave our misguided will without a possibility of rectification. When those who had transgressed the law inevitably received the death which had been decreed for the transgression, that death divided human life into two parts, this part in the body and the part hereafter outside of the body. The two parts do not have an equal measure of duration: the one is circumscribed by a very short limit of time, while the other extends into eternity.[6] The divine Providence gave us power because of His love for mankind to have each of these (I mean the good and the evil) in whichever we wish, either in this short and transient life or in those endless ages whose limit is infinity. But good and evil are named equivocally, and each of them has a double meaning (I mean in relation to the mind and the senses). Some people ascribe to the good part whatever seems pleasant to sense-perception, while others believe that only what appears to the mind both is good and should be so called. Those who have not trained their reasoning and have not examined what is better spend gluttonously in the fleshly life the share of good which is owed to their nature, saving up nothing for the life hereafter. But those who manage their life with critical reasoning and self-control, although in this short life they are distressed by those misfortunes which trouble the senses, yet store up good for the subsequent age, so that the better portion is extended for them throughout their eternal life. So this is the gulf, in my opinion, which does not come from the opening of the earth but is made by the decisions of human lives divided towards opposite choices. He who has definitively pursued pleasure for this life and has not cured his misguided choice by repentance makes the land of the good inaccessible to him hereafter. He digs for himself this impassable necessity, like an immense pit which

6 In Plato's *Republic*, Socrates compares the shortness of one
   lifetime with the unlimited duration of all time (608C).

cannot be crossed.

"For this reason also, I suppose, the good state of the soul in which the parable allows the athlete of endurance to rest is called the bosom of Abraham. We are told that this patriarch was the first of those who have ever lived to exchange the enjoyment of things present for the hope of things to come. When he had been stripped of everything in which his life consisted at the beginning, he had his abode in the lands of others, purchasing by his present suffering the good fortune for which he hoped. So just as we call a certain enclosed part of the sea figuratively a 'bosom,'[7] so the parable seems to me to signify the evidence of those immeasurable good things by the name of a 'bosom' in which all those who sail virtuously through the present life, when they depart from here, moor their souls as if in a calm harbor. For the others, however, the deprivation of the things which they consider good becomes a flame burning the soul, which needs but does not obtain a drop from that sea of good things which surges around the holy ones.

"As for the tongue, the eye, the finger, and the rest of the corporeal names in this dialogue of incorporeal souls, when you look at them you will admit that they are in accord with the interpretation which we have worked out by conjecture concerning the soul, if you consider the intention of the words. As the concurrence of the elements creates the essence of the body as a whole, so it is likely that the nature of the parts in the body is completed by the same cause. So if the soul is still present to the elements from the body when they have been mixed into the universe, it will not merely recognize and remain in the full complement of the elements which came together into the whole structure. It will remember also the particular construction of each of the parts; it will know which portions of the elements were used to complete our limbs. It is not at all improbable that the soul which is in the whole complement of

7   Greek κόλπος can refer both to the bosom or lap of a human
     being and to a bay or cove of the sea.

the elements is also in the elements of each part. Thus if we look at the elements in which the particular limbs of the body exist potentially, supposing that the Scripture is referring to these in saying that the finger is with the soul, as well as the eye and the tongue and all the other parts, after the dissolution of the structure, we shall not depart from what is probable. So if each item leads the mind away from a corporeal understanding of the narrative, surely it is likely that this Hades also which has just been mentioned is not intended to signify a place with that name. The Scripture must be teaching us that it is some invisible and incorporeal condition of life, in which the soul lives."[8]

8   Thus Macrina answers Gregory's question (above p. 61).

CHAPTER 6

The Purification of the Soul

"But in the story about the rich man and the poor man we also learn another doctrine which will have great relevance to our subject. The parable makes that man (the one who is subject to the passions and a lover of the flesh), when he sees that his misfortune is inescapable, show a concern for those who belong to his family on earth. Abraham says that the life of those who live in the flesh is not deprived of providence, but the guidance of the law and the prophets is available within their power of choice. Still the rich man continues to importune him on the grounds that the message may be convincing to them because of its unexpectedness if it is brought by someone returning to life from the dead."

"So then," I said, "what doctrine do we find in this?"

"The soul of Lazarus," she said, "is occupied with its present circumstances and does not turn toward anything which it has left behind. The rich man still sticks to the fleshly life as if with bird-lime which he has not thoroughly cleaned off even when he has ceased from life. He is still concerned with flesh and blood.[1] From the fact that he begs for those who share his family to be removed from evils, it is clear that he is not yet released from fleshly attachment. By this story," she said, "the Lord seems to be teaching that we who are living in the flesh ought as much as

1   This section is modelled on a passage in Plato's *Phaedo* (81A-D), where Socrates speaks of souls which are contaminated by attachment to bodily pleasures and cannot escape to the invisible divine world after death. Macrina, however, replaces the word "body" with "flesh" in the Pauline sense of sinful human nature (body and soul).

possible to separate ourselves and release ourselves from its hold by the life of virtue, so that after death we may not need another death to cleanse us from the remains of the fleshly glue. Then, as if chains have been broken away from the soul, its course may become light and easy towards the good, when no bodily weight drags the soul to itself. So if one should become completely carnal in his mind, devoting all the activity and energy of his soul to the will of the flesh,[2] such a man even when he gets out of the flesh is not separated from its experiences. Those who spend most of their time in evil-smelling places, even if they go out into the fresh air, are not cleansed from the unpleasantness which has adhered to them from prolonged contact. In the same way, even when the transition has been made to the invisible and rarified life, the lovers of the flesh would doubtless be unable to avoid bringing with them some of the fleshly odor. This makes their pangs more grievous, as their soul has become partly materialized from such an environment. There seems to be some support for this opinion in what certain people say, that often around the bodies' graves there appear some kind of shadowy shapes of the departed.[3] If this really happens, it proves that the soul has become more attached than it should be to the present fleshly life, so that even when it is driven out of the flesh it is not willing to fly clean away. It does not even allow its form to be completely changed into invisibility, but stays with its shape even after its shape has been dissolved.[4] Although it has already gone outside of its shape, it wanders longingly in the material places and spends its time in them."

I kept silent a little while, thinking over the sense of what she had said. Then I said, "It seems to me that some discrepancy arises between what you have said just now and what we examined earlier

2   Compare John 1:13.
3   Plato, *Phaedo* 81D.
4   The idea that the shape may not completely disappear after death comes from a pagan belief that the soul after death retains a ghostly kind of body.

concerning the emotions. If such impulses of the soul are considered to operate in us because of our relationship with the irrational animals, impulses which our discussion enumerated previously, namely anger, fear, desire, pleasure, and the like—we said that the good use of these is virtue, but through their defective use evil comes about.[5] Besides, we discussed the contribution of each of the other passions to the virtuous life and in particular the fact that we are led to God by desire. We are drawn upwards towards Him as if by a rope. The discussion seems somehow to be working against our purpose," I said.

"What do you mean?" she asked.

"I mean that if every irrational impulse in us is quenched after our purification, not even the desiring impulse will exist at all. If this should not exist, there would not even be a yearning for the better, since the soul would not retain the kind of movement which could arouse it toward the appetite for good things."

"To this we reply," she said, "that the faculty of contemplation and discernment is proper to the godlike part of the soul, since by these we comprehend even the divine.[6] So, you see, if our soul should become free of its attachment to the irrational emotions either by our effort in this life or by the purification hereafter, it will in no way be hindered from the contemplation of the beautiful. For beauty has in its own nature an attractiveness for everyone who looks at it. So if the soul becomes clean of all evil, it will exist entirely in beauty. The divine is beautiful by its own nature. The soul will be joined with the divine through its purity, adhering to that which is proper to it. If this should happen, there will no longer be a need for the impulse of desire to lead us toward the beautiful. He who passes his life in darkness will desire the light; if he should come into the light, attainment will replace desire. The possibility of attainment makes desire useless and vain.

5   See above p. 60.
6   See above p. 54.

Therefore the soul will not receive any disadvantage in respect to participation in the good, if it should be freed from these impulses. It will go back to itself and see clearly what it is in its nature, and through its own beauty it will look upon the archetype as if in a mirror and an image. We can truly say that the accurate likeness of the divine[7] consists in our soul's imitation of the superior Nature.

"That Nature which is above all understanding, located far beyond what appears in us, leads its own life in another manner, not as we are now in our way of living; for we human beings are carried wherever the impulse of our choice goes, because our nature is always entirely in motion. The soul is not disposed in the same way in its forward direction (as one might say) and in the reverse. Hope initiates the forward motion, but memory takes over the guidance as the motion goes forwards towards hope. If hope should lead the soul towards that which is good by nature, the motion of choice marks a bright track on the memory. But if the soul is deceived of the good, because hope has tricked it with some imitation of beauty, the memory which follows the experiences turns into shame.[8] And thus this civil war is established in the soul, in which memory fights with hope, accusing it of guiding our choice badly. The feeling of shame clearly interprets some such meaning, when the soul is stung by the result. The soul attacks the thoughtless impulse with repentance as if with a whip and enlists forgetfulness as an ally against the source of grief.

"But because our nature is impoverished of the beautiful, it always reaches towards that which it needs.[9] This appetite for what is lacking is the desiring condition of our nature, which is either foiled of the truly beautiful through misjudgment or perhaps even obtains by chance that which is good to obtain. But the Nature which exceeds every good

7   Genesis 1:26.
8   This discussion of shame, with mention of a whip, reminds us
     again of the chariot myth in Plato's *Phaedrus* (254A ff.).
9   In Plato's *Symposium* (201B), Socrates asserts that Love (Ἔρως)
     is always needy.

conception and surpasses every power,[10] because It needs none of those things which are thought of as good, being Itself the fullness of good things, and because It is not in beauty by participation of some beauty,[11] but is Itself the nature of the beautiful (whatever the mind may assume the beautiful to be), does not even admit the impulse of hope in Itself, for hope operates only in respect to what is not present. 'Why does one still hope for what he has?' says the apostle.[12] Neither does It need the activity of memory to understand the things which are, for that which is seen does not need to be remembered. Since, then, the divine Nature surpasses every good, and the good is dear in every way to the good, for this reason, looking at Itself, It both wants what It has and has what It wants, not receiving anything from outside into Itself. But nothing is outside It, except evil only, which (paradoxical though this may be), has its being in non-being; for there is no other origin of evil but the deprivation of being.[13] That which may properly be said to exist is the nature of the good. So that which is not in true existence must be in non-existence.

"Since, then, the soul becomes godlike when it has put off all the varied impulses of its nature, and when it has passed beyond desire it has entered into that towards which it was previously being raised by desire, it no longer gives any place in itself either to hope or to memory. It has what it was hoping for, and it drives out memory from its mind in its occupation with the enjoyment of good things. Thus it imitates the superior life, being conformed to the properties of the divine Nature, so that nothing else is left to it

10 Compare Ephesians 3:19, Philippians 4:7.
11 Macrina equates God with the Form of the Beautiful. According to Plato, material things are beautiful by participation in this ideal Form (see *Symposium* 211B, *Phaedo* 100C).
12 Romans 8:24.
13 The idea that evil is deprivation of being arose among Neoplatonists; see Origen, *Commentary on John 2.13*.92-96, and Plotinus, *Enneads* 1.8.3. The Christian Origen and the pagan Plotinus studied under the same teacher at Alexandria.

but the disposition of love, as it becomes attached in its nature to the beautiful. This is love, the interior attachment to that which is pleasing. So when the soul which has become simple and uniform and an accurate image of God finds that truly simple and immaterial good, the one thing which is really lovable and desirable, it attaches itself to it and combines with it through the impulse and operation of love. It conforms itself to that which is always being grasped and found, and becomes through its likeness to the good that which the nature is in which it participates. If the soul has no desire because it has no lack of any good thing, it would follow that the soul which has no insufficiency also casts out from itself the desiring impulse and disposition, which occurs only when something wanted is not present. The divine apostle introduced us to this doctrine also, when he predicted a cessation and conclusion of all our eager efforts, even those which are directed towards the good, but of love only he did not find a limit: for he says, 'Prophecies will pass away, and knowledge will pass away, but love never ends,' which is equivalent to being always the same.[14] But when he says that faith and hope remain along with love, again he rightly puts love ahead of the others;[15] for hope acts so long as the enjoyment of what is hoped for is not present, and faith in the same way becomes a support for the uncertainty of the things hoped for. This is how he defined it when he said, 'Faith is the assurance of things hoped for.'[16] But when the thing hoped for comes, all the others grow quiet while the operation of love remains, not finding anything to take its place. For this reason also it has the primacy among all virtuous actions as well as among the commandments of the law.[17] So if the soul should ever reach this goal, it will have no need of the others, as it embraces the fullness of existing things and seems somehow alone to pre-

14 1 Corinthians 13:8.
15 1 Corinthians 13:13.
16 Hebrews 11:1.
17 Matthew 22:37-40.

serve in itself the impression of divine blessedness. For the life of
the superior nature is love, since the beautiful is in every respect
lovable for those who know it, and the Divine knows Itself. But
knowledge becomes love, because that which is known is beautiful by nature. Insolent satiety does not touch the truly beautiful.[18]
Since satiety does not cut off the attachment of love to the
beautiful, the divine life will always operate through love, the
divine life which is beautiful by nature and from its nature is
lovingly disposed towards the beautiful. There is no limit to the
operation of love, since the beautiful has no limit, so that love
might cease with the limit of the beautiful. The beautiful is limited
only by its opposite. But whatever by its nature cannot admit
anything worse will proceed towards the limitless and unbounded
good."

18 Origen said that souls entered into bodies when they became
    sated with the heavenly life: *On first principles* 1.3.8; 2.9.2.

CHAPTER 7

Why Is Purification Painful?

"Since, therefore, every nature tends to attract what is proper to it, and the human is in some way proper to God, because it bears in itself the imitation of its Archetype, necessarily the soul is attracted to the Divine which is related to it (for what is proper to God must come safely to Him). But if the soul is light and simple, with no bodily weight holding it down, its progress towards the One who attracts it becomes pleasant and easy.[1] If, on the contrary, it is fastened to the material condition with the nails of passionate attachment,[2] it will probably experience something like what happens to the bodies which are buried by debris when buildings collapse in earthquakes. Imagine, for example, that these bodies are not only weighed down by fallen debris, but also are pierced by some spits or stakes which are found in the pile. Whatever bodies in this condition are likely to endure when they are dragged out by their relatives from the collapse for funeral rites (they will be all mangled and torn, and will suffer whatever is most painful, as the debris and the nails lacerate them because of the force of those who pull them out)—some such experience I think will happen to the soul, when the divine Power by Its love for mankind draws Its own out from the irrational and material debris. For it is not out of hatred or vengeance for an evil life (in my opinion) that God brings painful conditions upon sinners, when He seeks after and draws to Himself whatever has come to birth for His sake; but for a better purpose He draws the soul to Himself, who is the fountain of all blessedness. The painful

1   See above p.76; compare Wisdom 9:15.
2   Nails attach the soul to the body in Plato's *Phaedo* (83D).

condition necessarily happens as an incidental consequence to the
one who is drawn. When goldsmiths purify gold by fire from the
matter which is mixed with it, they do not only melt the adulterant in
the fire, but inevitably the pure metal is melted along with the base
admixture. When the latter is consumed the former remains. In the
same way when evil is consumed by the purifying fire, the soul
which is united to evil must necessarily also be in the fire until the
base adulterant material is removed, consumed by the fire. Or if
particularly sticky mud is plastered thickly around a rope, then the
end of the rope is led through some small space, and some one pulls
forcibly on the end of the rope towards the inside, necessarily the
rope must follow the one who pulls, but the plastered mud must
remain outside of the hole scraped off the rope by the forcible
pulling. Because of the mud the rope does not move forward easily,
but has to be pulled hard. Something like this I think we should
imagine for the state of the soul. Wrapped up as it is in material and
earthly attachments, it struggles and is stretched, as God draws His
own to Himself. What is alien to God has to be scraped off forcibly
because it has somehow grown onto the soul. This is the cause of the
sharp and unbearable pains which the soul must endure."

"So the divine judgment," I said, "as it seems, does not primarily bring punishment on sinners. As our discourse has just shown,
it operates only by separating good from evil and pulling the soul
towards the fellowship of blessedness. It is the tearing apart of what
has grown together which brings pain to the one who is being
pulled."

"This is my opinion too," said my teacher. "I also think that the
measure of pain is proportional to the quantity of evil in each
person. For it is not likely that the one who has gone far in forbidden
evils and the one who has fallen into moderate transgressions will
be distressed equally as they are purified from their wretched
condition. Probably that painful fire is kindled more or less hotly
depending on the quantity of matter, and it burns as long as it has

fuel. So if a person's material burden is great, the consuming flame must also become great and long-lasting; but if someone is exposed to the consuming fire more briefly, the punishment relaxes its severe and piercing operation in proportion to the smaller measure of evil in the subject. For evil must be altogether removed in every way from being, and, as we have said before, that which does not really exist must cease to exist at all. Since evil does not exist by its nature outside of free choice, when all choice is in God, evil will suffer a complete annihilation because no receptacle remains for it."

"But what is the benefit of this good hope," I asked, "for the person who considers how great an evil it is to endure even one year of pain? If that unendurable pain is extended to the length of this whole age, what consolation may a person gain from the hope for afterwards, if his punishment lasts as long as the age?"

"This is why we must take care," my teacher said, "either to keep our soul altogether pure and free from fellowship with evil, or, if this is utterly impossible because of our passionate nature, to limit our failures in virtue as much as possible to moderate lapses which are easily cured. The Gospel teaching knows a certain debtor of ten thousand talents,[3] one of five hundred denarii and another of fifty,[4] and one of a quadrans, which is the smallest coin.[5] The just judgment of God pursues all and adjusts the necessary recompense to equal the gravity of the debt, without overlooking even the least. The Gospel says that the restitution for the debt is not made by payment of money, but that the debtor is handed over 'to the torturers until,' it says, 'he pays back all that he owes.'[6] This means simply that by the torment he pays the necessary obligation, the debt of participation in distress which he

3 Matthew 18:24.
4 Luke 7:41.
5 Matthew 5:26.
6 Matthew 18:34.

incurred during his life by foolishly choosing pleasure straight and unmixed with its opposite. When he has thus put away all that is alien to him (which is sin) and taken off the shameful garment of his debts, he enters into freedom and confidence. Freedom consists in becoming like that which has no master and is under its own control. This likeness was given to us by God at the beginning, but has been veiled by the shame of our debts. All freedom is one in nature and belongs together. Consequently, therefore, everything which is free will be joined with its like. Virtue has no master. Therefore everything free will be in virtue, for that which is free also has no master. But indeed the divine Nature is the source of all virtue. Hence those who are released from evil will be in the divine Nature, so that, as the apostle says, 'God may be all in all.'[7] This word, which says that God becomes all and in all, seems to me to confirm clearly the idea which we have examined previously. For while we carry on our present life in many different ways, there are many things in which we participate, such as time, air, place, food and drink, clothing, sun, lamplight, and many other necessities of life, of which none is God. The blessedness which we await, however, does not need any of these, but the divine Nature will become everything for us and will replace everything, distributing itself appropriately for every need of that life. This is clear from the divine sayings, that God becomes a place for the saints,[8] a house,[9] a garment,[10] nourishment, drink,[11] light,[12] wealth,[13] dominion,[14] and every concept and name of the things which contribute to the good life for us. He who becomes all will also be in all. In this the

7   1 Corinthians 15:28.
8   Perhaps John 15:4.
9   Perhaps Ephesians 2:20-22.
10   Galatians 3:27.
11   John 6:35, 53-56.
12   John 8:12; Revelation 21:23; 22:5.
13   Perhaps Matthew 19:21, Revelation 3:18.
14   Perhaps Matthew 19:28-29, Revelation 3:21.

apostle seems to me to teach the complete annihilation of evil. If God will be in everything which exists, evil obviously will not be among the things which exist; for if one should suppose that evil existed, how would it remain true that God is 'in all'? If evil is excluded, not all things are included. But He who will be 'in all' will not be in what does not exist."

"So what should we say," I asked, "to those who lack courage to bear their misfortunes?"

"We should talk to them like this," my teacher said. "'Dear people, it is useless for you to grumble and complain at the necessary order and sequence of events. You do not know towards what goal each part in the universe is being directed, because everything must be united to the divine Nature in a certain order and sequence according to the skillful wisdom of the Governor. Our rational nature came to birth for this purpose, so that the wealth of divine good things might not be idle. A kind of vessels and voluntary receptacles for souls were fashioned by the Wisdom which constructed the universe, in order that there should be a container to receive good things, a container which would always become larger with the addition of what would be poured into it. For the participation in the divine good is such that it makes anyone into whom it enters greater and more receptive. As it is taken up it increases the power and magnitude of the recipient, so that the person who is nourished always grows and never ceases from growth. Since the fountain of good things flows unfailingly, the nature of the participants who use all the influx to add to their own magnitude (because nothing of what is received is superfluous or useless) becomes at the same time both more capable of attracting the better and more able to contain it. Each adds to the other: the one who is nourished gains greater power from the abundance of good things, and the nourishing supply rises in flood to match the increase of the one who is growing. Those whose growth is not cut off by any limit will surely continue to increase in this manner. Then, when such prospects lie before us, do you complain because nature proceeds by the road which is ordained for us towards its proper goal? Otherwise our course cannot reach those good things, if we have not shaken off from our soul this heaviness which weighs us down (I mean this earthly burden). Unless we have been cleansed by better pursuits from the attachment to it which we have acquired in this life, we cannot be united in purity to that which we resemble. But if you have some fondness for this body, and you are sorry to be unyoked from what you love, do not be in despair about this either. For although this bodily covering is now dissolved by death, you will see it woven again from the same elements, not indeed with its present coarse and heavy texture, but with the thread respun into something subtler and lighter, so that the beloved body may be with you and be restored to you again in better and even more lovable beauty.' "

"Somehow," I said, "the sequence of our discussion appears to have brought us to the doctrine of the resurrection, which seems to me, on the basis of scriptural teaching, to be true, trustworthy, and indubitable. But since the weakness of human thought relies more on comprehensible reasoning to establish a conviction of this kind, it would be well not to let this topic go by without consideration. So let us reflect on what we ought to say."

CHAPTER 8

Transmigration of Souls

My teacher said, "Those outside our philosophy by various assumptions in different ways have partly attained to the doctrine of the resurrection.[1] Although they do not agree fully with our teachers, still they do not altogether lack this hope. Some do violence to humanity by association, when they assert that the same soul becomes in turn that of a man and that of a beast.[2] They say that it puts on different bodies and keeps passing over into what pleases it, becoming either a winged or an aquatic or a terrestrial animal after the human; and again from these bodies it returns to the human nature. Others extend this nonsense even to the shrubbery, so as to think that even the arboreal life is appropriate and fitting for the soul.[3] Others accept only this much, that another human being always receives the soul from a human being and that the same souls are always leading the human life, as they keep entering now into these men, now again into others. But we say that it is best to start from the teachings of the Church and to accept from those philosophers only enough to demonstrate that they are in partial agreement with the doctrine of the resurrection. Insofar as they say that the souls are reintroduced into certain

1 The doctrine of reincarnation or transmigration of souls seems to have been taught by Pythagoras and his followers, by Empedocles, and later by Plato.
2 In the myth of Er (*Republic* X), Plato describes souls choosing to be reincarnated as human beings and animals.
3 According to Empedocles, the greatest souls are successively incarnated among animals as lions, among plants as laurel trees, and among men as prophets, poets, physicians, and princes (fr. 127, 146, 147).

bodies after they are unyoked from their present bodies, their view does not differ too much from the return to life for which we hope. Our discussion says that the body is constituted now and will be reconstituted later from the elements of the cosmos. The outsiders' ideas are equivalent, for they could not imagine that the nature of the body is established in any other way than by the concurrence of the elements. Our ideas differ to this extent, however: we say that the same body is constructed again around the same soul, fitted together from the same elements; but they suppose that the soul migrates to another body, with or without reason and sense-perception. They agree that the body is constituted from the parts of the cosmos; they differ because they do not believe that it is constituted from the same parts which became attached to the soul at the beginning of the fleshly life. Therefore let pagan philosophy bear witness that it is not implausible for the soul to enter again into the body.

"But now it may be time for us to examine the inconsistency of their teaching, and by the very sequence which emerges in the course of our reasoning to reveal the truth as far as possible. So what should we say about these matters? Those who settle the soul in diverse natures seem to me to confuse the properties of the nature. They mix all things up and confound them with one another, the irrational, the rational, the sensate and insensate—if these properties occur with each other, and are not separated from each other by any natural orderliness which would prevent them from crossing over. For when these people say that the same soul now becomes rational and intelligent through being wrapped in our kind of a body, and again burrows with the serpents, or flocks with the birds, or carries burdens, or devours flesh, or lives under water, or even migrates to the insensate beings, taking root and growing into a tree, and sprouting branches, and on these producing either flower, or thorn, or some nourishing or harmful fruit, it is just as if they judged everything to be the same and the nature of all beings to be one, mixed in a confused and undifferentiated association with itself, with no property distinguishing one thing from the other. For he who says that the same entity enters into everything can mean only that everything is one, if the apparent difference of beings in no way hinders the mixing of unrelated things.[4] It would follow necessarily that even if a man sees a game animal or a carnivore, he must consider that the beast is related to him.[5] Such a man will regard the poisonous hemlock as similar in nature to himself, if indeed he sees humanity even in the plants;[6] and he will distrust even the grapes which are raised for the benefit of our life. After all, this is also one of the things which grow; another kind of plant is the sprouts of grain by which we are nourished. So how will he bring the sickle to cut the grain? How will he press the grapes, or uproot the thorns from his field, or pluck the flower, or hunt the birds, or light a fire of wood, if he does not know whether he is raising his hand against relatives, or ancestors, or fellow tribesmen, and kindling the fire with their bodies, or mixing the winebowl, or preparing nourishment? If he supposes that through each of these incarnations the soul of man becomes plant or animal, but that no signs are marked on them to show which plant or animal is from a human being, and which comes into being otherwise, the man who is prejudiced by such an assumption will be disposed in the same way towards all things. He will necessarily either be harsh against the very men who appear in human form; or, if he should incline to natural kindness towards those related to him, he will be disposed similarly towards every living thing, whether it

4   Aristotle rejects Pythagorean theories of transmigration on the
    ground that each kind of soul needs to have the right kind of
    body (*On the soul* 407B 22-26).
5   The Pythagoreans may have practiced vegetarianism for this
    reason.
6   By reminding us of Socrates' death, the mention of hemlock
    reinforces the parallelism between this dialogue and Plato's
    Phaedo.

is among the snakes or among the beasts. Even if he comes into a forest of trees, the man who has accepted this doctrine will think that the trees are a people of human beings. So what will be the life of such a man, since he must either be cautious towards everything because all are related to him, or be harsh even towards mankind because they are not distinguished from the other species? Therefore we must reject such a theory from our discourse.[7]

"Many other reasons also logically lead us away from such a hypothesis. I have heard about those who promote such ideas, that they imagine some tribes of souls living in their own common-wealth before the life in the body, revolving with the rotation of the universe in the subtlety and mobility of their nature.[8] By a certain inclination towards evil the souls lose their wings and enter into bodies, first into human bodies; then, because of the association with the irrational passions, after their departure from human life they become beasts. Thereafter they decline as far as the vegetative and insensate life. These people say in effect that the soul which is naturally subtle and mobile first becomes heavy and downward-tending, settling in human bodies because of its wickedness. Then, when the logical power has been extinguished, it lives in the irrational animals. Finally, when even the grace of sense-perception has been removed, it partakes in the insensate life which is in plants. From this again it ascends through the same steps and is reestablished in the heavenly place. Such a doctrine is refuted for those who understand even moderately how to judge by the very fact that it is inconsistent with itself; for if the soul is dragged down from the life of heaven because of evil to the material life, and from this climbs up again to the heavenly life because of virtue, their theory turns out to be ignorant, which should be considered more honor-

7   Macrina rejects transmigration on practical rather than logical grounds; the hypothesis would make life absurdly difficult.
8   Macrina seems to be thinking of Plato's *Republic* (the myth of Er). Her criticism of theories about the fall of the soul would apply also to Origen's *On first principles*.

able, the material or the heavenly life. The soul seems to keep going around a kind of circle, always being unstable wherever it is. If it goes from the bodiless life to the bodily, and from this to the insensate, and from there ascends again to the bodiless, those who teach these things are imagining nothing but an undifferentiated confusion of evils and goods. For the heavenly life does not remain in blessedness, if indeed evil takes hold of those who live there; nor is matter without its share of virtue, if indeed they think that the soul ascends again from here to the good, but from there begins the life of evil. They say that the soul revolving around the heaven becomes involved in evil, and when it has been dragged down to the material life by evil, it is raised up again from here to the life on high. They are paradoxically asserting that material life purifies souls from evil but the undeviating circuit of heaven is the source and cause of evil—if indeed when the souls grow wings through virtue they travel from here on high, but from there when their wings have fallen off through evil they become ground-seeking and earth-dwelling, mingled with the density of the material nature.[9]

"The absurdity of such doctrines does not end with this reversal of their assumptions, but not even their own thoughts remain fixed permanently. For if they call the heavenly 'immutable,' how does passion have a place in the immutable? And if the lower nature is subject to passion, how does freedom from passions arise in the passionate nature? But they mix up the immiscible and unite the incompatible. They see immutability in passion and again passionlessness in mutability, and neither always remaining in the same condition. In the very place from which they banished the soul for its wickedness, they settle it again as into a life secure and pure from materiality, as if forgetting that from there the soul was dragged down by evil so that it became mixed with the lower nature. So the disparagement of this life and the

9   The image of souls losing their wings and growing them again comes from Plato's *Phaedrus*.

praise of the heavenly are confused with each other and mixed up. Their opinion attributes goodness to the inferior life, and the supposedly better life gives the soul a start in its inclination to the worse. Therefore every deceptive and inconsistent idea about these matters must be rejected from the teaching of the truth. Moreover, we must not follow even those who say that souls migrate from men to men, and that women come into being again from women, not to mention those who think that souls from female bodies migrate into a masculine life, or conversely that souls separated from male bodies enter into women. All of these miss the truth.

"The first theory[10] must be rejected not only because it is unstable and deceptive, reversing its own assumptions, but also because it is impious, asserting that nothing that exists is brought into being unless evil gives a beginning to its nature. If neither human beings, nor plants, nor cattle grow unless a soul falls from above on them, and the fall comes through evil, then these people must suppose that evil begins the constitution of the things that exist. How does it happen that at the same time a human being grows out of marriage, and the fall of the souls coincides with the eagerness for marriage? And what is even more unreasonable than this, if in spring many of the irrational creatures mate, then can we say that spring makes evil develop in the heavenly sphere, so that at the same time souls happen to fall as they become filled with evil and the bellies of animals happen to conceive? What would one say about the farmer who fixes in the earth the seedlings of plants? How could his hand bury the human soul along with the plant, as the soul's loss of wings coincides with the man's impulse for planting?

"The other opinion[11] is equally absurd, moreover—the idea that the soul meddles with the intercourse of those who live in wedlock or watches their childbed, in order to enter into bodies which are being born. But if the husband should repudiate the

10 That human souls migrate into plants and animals.
11 That human souls migrate only into human bodies.

marriage, and the wife should free herself from the necessity of labor, will evil then not weigh down the soul? Does marriage give to the evil above the signal to attack the souls, or even without marriage does the attachment to evil take hold of the soul? In that case the soul will wander like a homeless refugee in a kind of Limbo, because it has fallen away from the heavenly life but has not yet obtained the lot of a body for a receptacle, if this is how it happens. Furthermore, how will they imagine that the divine is in charge of the things which exist, if they attribute the beginning of human life to this accidental and irrational fall of the soul? For it is entirely necessary that what comes after be in accord with the beginning; that is to say, if life began from some automatic coincidence, its conclusion also must happen by chance. It is nonsense for such people to attribute existing things to divine power, if they do not say that the things in the universe come into being by divine will, but assign the beginnings of the things which come into existence to some evil accident, as if our human life would not have been established if evil had not given the signal for life to start. So if the beginning of life is like this, obviously also that which follows will continue in accord with the beginning. For no one would say that good grows from evil, or evil from good, but we expect the fruit to be produced in accordance with the nature of the seed.

"Therefore an automatic and fortuitous impulse will govern all of life, if no providence pervades what exists. Besides, rational foresight will be altogether useless, virtue will have no benefit, and remaining unacquainted with evil will be of no value. For everything will be entirely in the power of chance, and life will be just like ships without ballast, driven hither and thither by fortuitous accidents as if by waves, now to a good and again to a worthless outcome. It is not possible for the benefit which comes from virtue to develop in those whose nature has its beginning from the opposite. If our life is divinely directed, we must also agree that evil does not begin our life; but if we come into being through evil, in every way we will live entirely according to it. So this will make nonsense of the judgment after this life, and the recompense for deserts, and whatever else we say and believe in the hope of eliminating evil. For how is it possible for the man who has come into being through evil to escape from it? How would man make a start towards choosing the virtuous life, if his nature gets its principle from evil, as they say? None of the irrational beasts attempts to speak like a human being. They use the voice which is innate and natural to them and consider it no misfortune to be lacking in speech. In the same way also, if men are thought to have evil as the source and cause of their life, they could not even begin to desire virtue, because it would be outside their nature.

"But in fact all those who have purified their souls by reason have a zeal and desire for the virtuous life. So this clearly proves that evil is not older than life, nor did it provide the first principles for our nature. Instead, our life is governed by the wisdom of God which directs the universe. When the soul has come to birth in the manner which pleases the Creator, then by its free will it chooses that which accords with its inclination, becoming whatever it wishes by its power of choice. We could learn this from the example of our eyes: sight comes from nature, but non-seeing from choice or accident. What is contrary to nature may occur at some time instead of what is natural, if one either voluntarily closes the eyes or by some accident is deprived of sight. Thus we can say both that the constitution of the soul is from God and (since we do not conceive of any evil in connection with the Divine) that the soul is free from the necessity of evil. When it comes into existence in this manner it is led by its own inclination to what seems good to it. It may live in the darkness of deception, closing its eyes to the good by choice, or by a plot of the enemy which besets our life suffering an injury to its eyes; or else looking in purity towards the truth, it may move far away from the passions of darkness."

CHAPTER 9

The Origin of the Soul

"Someone will ask, 'When did the soul come into being, and how?' But we must entirely remove from our discourse the inquiry concerning how each thing has come into being. Not even concerning those things which are close at hand for our knowledge, things which we comprehend through our senses, could a rational investigation conceive how that which appears was established; such matters are not considered comprehensible even by holy and divinely-inspired men. For 'By faith we understand,' says the apostle, 'that the ages have been fashioned by the word of God, so that what is seen is not made out of things which appear.'[1] He would not have said that, I suppose, if he had thought that the explanation could be found by reason. The apostle says that he has believed this much, that the age itself was fashioned by the divine will, and whatever has come to be within it (whatever this 'age' may be, in which is comprehended all the visible and invisible creation); but the *how* he has left unexamined. For I do not think this is attainable by those who seek, as the investigation of these matters presents many difficulties to us. How from the stationary nature does that which moves arise?[2] How does the dimensional and composite arise from the simple and dimensionless? Does it come from the superior Nature itself? We must deny this, because existing beings are different in kind from that Na-

1 Hebrews 11:3. Macrina could also have mentioned Socrates' rejection of natural science, described in Plato's *Phaedo*.
2 Aristotle was particularly concerned to account for the origin of motion, which is why he posited a Prime Mover. Generally Macrina is referring to Aristotelian concerns in this section.

ture. Then from somewhere else? But indeed reason does not see anything outside of the divine Nature. We would be assuming multiple first principles if we should posit anything outside of the creative cause, from which the skillful wisdom borrows the means for the creation. So since existing beings have only one cause, but the things which the superior Nature brings into existence are not of the same kind as It, both hypotheses are equally absurd, whether we suppose that the creation is from the nature of God or that everything subsists from some other essence. For we would have to imagine that divinity was among the properties of the created world, if what comes to being were of the same kind as God; or else we would posit some material nature outside the divine Essence which would be equal with God in unbegottenness because its being would also be eternal. In fact the presumptuous Manicheans, as well as some people who accept equivalent ideas from pagan philosophy, have made this fantasy their doctrine.[3]

"In order to avoid as much as possible the absurdity of each position in the inquiry about existing beings, we shall follow the example of the apostle and refrain from meddling with the discussion concerning how each thing exists. We shall indicate in passing only this much, that the impulse of divine choice, when it wishes, becomes a thing. Its plan is realized and immediately becomes a nature. Whatever the almighty Power wishes wisely and skillfully, Its will is not made ineffective. But the realization of the will is essence. Now beings are divided into two kinds, the intellectual and the corporeal. The creation of intellectual beings does not seem to be in any way incompatible with the nature of the Incorporeal One. They seem related to that Nature in presenting invisibility, intangibility, and dimensionlessness. One would be right to assume that all these qualities apply to the superior Nature also. But because the

3   Pagan Greek philosophers generally assumed that there was some eternally existing matter from which the universe was formed.

corporeal creation appears with properties which are not shared
with the Divine, our discussion encounters a particularly great
difficulty if we are not able to see how the visible arises from the
invisible, the solid and hard from the intangible, the limited from
the unlimited, from the unquantifiable and immeasurable that
which is entirely bounded by some measures related to quantity,
as well as each property which we understand in connection with
the corporeal nature. Concerning these we say this much: that
nothing of what appears in relation to the body is body in itself,
not shape, nor color, nor weight, nor dimension, nor quantity, nor
anything else of what is related to quality, but each of these is a
principle. The concurrence and union of these with one another
becomes a body.[4] So since the qualities which together complete
the body are comprehended by mind and not by sense-perception,
and the Divine is intellectual, why should not the Intelligible One
be able to create the intelligible qualities which by their concurrence with one another have engendered the nature of our bodies?

"But enough of this digression. What we were asking was
this: if the souls do not subsist before the bodies, when and how
do they come to be? Our discourse has refrained from meddling
with the inquiry concerning the *how*, because we suppose the
answer to be unattainable. We must still consider *when* the souls
have the beginning of their existence. Our answer will follow
from what we have examined previously. For if we should grant
that the soul lives in some particular condition before the body,
we would necessarily have to allow that there is some force in
those absurd invented doctrines which settle the souls in the
bodies through evil. On the other hand, no one with good sense
would imagine that the origin of the souls is later and younger than
the formation of the bodies, since everyone knows that none of the

4   Macrina is denying the materiality of matter! This is how
    Gregory (and Basil also) avoided positing a prime matter
    which would have existed before God's creation of the world.

soulless beings has in itself the power of movement and growth.[5]
But there is no disagreement or doubt that those which are being
nourished in the womb have growth and spatial movement.

"So the remaining alternative is to suppose that soul and body
have one and the same beginning. Just as, when the earth receives
from the farmer a slip cut off from its root, it produces a tree, not
itself putting the power of growth into that which it nourishes, but
only giving the start towards growth to the slip which is planted; in
the same way we say that what is separated from a human being for
the propagation of a human being is itself also in some way a
soul-endowed being from a soul-endowed being, a growing being
from a growing being. If the cutting was too short to contain all the
energies and motions of the soul, we should not be at all surprised.
The seed of grain does not appear immediately as an ear (for how
would it contain so much in so little?), but as the earth nurses it with
appropriate food, the grain becomes an ear, not changing its nature
while it is in the soil but revealing and perfecting itself by the
operation of its nourishment. So just as the growth of a sprouting
seed proceeds gradually to its goal, in the same manner also when
a human being is formed the power of the soul appears according
to the measure of the bodily stature. First the power enters into the
embryo which is formed within the womb through the capacity for
receiving nourishment and growing, but afterwards it brings the
grace of sense-perception to the infant which comes forth into light.
Then, as an adult plant produces fruit, it gradually reveals the
faculty of reason, not all at once, but increasing along with the
growth of the child in the normal order of development. Indeed that
which is separated from soul-endowed beings for the constitution
of a soul-endowed being cannot be dead (for deadness comes about
by deprivation of soul, and lacking would not lead to having).
Therefore we understand that a common transition into being takes

5   The word ἄψυχος literally "soulless," regularly means "inani-
    mate." Likewise ἔμψυχος means "animate, alive."

place for the compound constituted from both soul and body. The one does not go before, nor the other come later.

"But logic necessarily foresees that the number of souls will eventually cease to grow, so that nature may not flow on forever, always pouring onward through successors, and never ceasing from movement.[6] But I suppose that the reason why even our nature must become stable at some time is this: when all the intellectual creation stops at its proper fulfillment, it is likely that mankind also will reach a limit; for as humanity is not dissimilar to the rest of the intellectual creation, so it will not always appear to be deficient. The need continually to add successors implies that the nature is lacking something. So when mankind reaches its proper fulfillment, this streaming motion of our nature will entirely cease, because it has met its necessary limit. Then some other condition will receive our life, a different condition from that which we now experience in generation and corruption. For if there is no generation, inevitably there will be no corruption either. If composition goes before dissolution (we call 'composition' the transition through generation), we must undoubtedly infer that when composition does not lead, neither will dissolution follow. Therefore we have shown by logical argument that the life hereafter is stable and indissoluble, unchanged either by generation or by corruption."

6   Ancient mathematicians were unable to handle infinite sets, as we can see from the paradoxes of Zeno.

CHAPTER 10

The Doctrine of the Resurrection

After my teacher had explained this much, when most of the people sitting by thought that the discourse had reached a fitting conclusion, I for my part feared that there might not be anyone left to resolve for us the objections brought by outsiders concerning the resurrection, if the teacher should be overcome by her illness (as indeed it happened).

"Our discourse has not yet," I said, "grasped the most important point of the doctrines under investigation. For the inspired Scripture says, according to both the new and the old teaching, that as our nature proceeds in a certain order and series according to the periodic movement of time, there will eventually be a complete cessation of this flowing course which goes forward through the succession of descendants. When the fullness of the universe no longer allows increase in quantity, the whole complement of souls will return again from their invisible and scattered condition to unity and visibility. The same elements will come back to one another, returning in the same order as before. The Scriptures of the divine doctrine call this condition of life 'resurrection,' naming the whole movement of the elements from the upward rising of the earthly element."

"So what part of this," she asked, "has been omitted in what we have already said?"

"The actual doctrine of the resurrection," I said.[1]

"But surely," she said, "many of the matters which we have

1   We return after a rather lengthy digression to the issue raised above, p. 88.

discussed thoroughly are relevant to this goal."

"Don't you know," I said, "how great a swarm of objections our opponents bring forward against this hope?" At the same time I tried to tell her how many arguments are invented by contentious people to overthrow the doctrine of the resurrection.

But she said, "I think that we should first run briefly through what is set forth in various places by the divine Scripture concerning this doctrine, so that from there we may approach the conclusion of our discourse. I have heard, indeed, what David sings in his divine odes, when he has made the ordering of the universe the subject of his hymn. Near the end of the 103rd Psalm he says, 'You will take away their spirit, and they will die and return to their dust. You will send out Your Spirit, and they will be created, and You will renew the face of the earth.'[2] He is saying that the power of the Spirit, accomplishing everything in everything, both gives life to those whom it enters and removes from life those from whom it departs. He says that the death of the living happens by the departure of the Spirit, and by Its presence the renewal of the dead takes place. Because the death of those who are being renewed comes first in the order of the words, we can say that the mystery of the resurrection is being proclaimed to the Church, as David has foretold this grace by his spirit of prophecy.

"In another place, moreover, this same prophet says that the God of all, the Lord of those that are, has appeared to us to inaugurate the feast with a covering [of branches],[3] by the word 'covering' signifying the feast of the Tabernacles which was legislated of old by the tradition of Moses. Prophetically, I suppose, the lawgiver was foretelling what was to come: while the feast was always being celebrated, it had not yet been accomplished. Although the truth was being revealed in a type by the symbolism of what was being done, the true tabernacle had not

2   Psalm 103(104):29-30.
3   Psalm 117(118):27 (LXX).

yet been pitched.[4] According to the prophetic word, however, the
God and Lord of all revealed Himself to us in order to inaugurate
for human nature the feast of the tabernacle of our destroyed
dwelling, which would again be covered with a body when the
elements should come back together. For the word 'covering,'
according to its proper meaning, signifies a garment and the
adornment which this produces. But the verse of the psalm continues like this: 'God, the Lord, has even appeared to us; inaugurate a feast with a covering up to the horns of the altar.' This seems
to me to foretell symbolically that one feast is being established
for all the rational creation, the inferior joining together with the
superior in the assembly of the good. For in the symbolic arrangement of the Temple, not everyone was permitted to come inside
the outer walls, but all gentiles and foreigners were prohibited
from entry. Again, not all of those who came inside had an equal
right to enter further, unless they had been sanctified by a purer
manner of life and certain cleansing rites. Furthermore, even
among these very people the interior part of the Temple was not
accessible to all, but the priests alone were designated to enter
within the curtain as their priestly service might require. Moreover, the hidden and inaccessible part of the Temple in which the
altar was located, decorated with horns surrounding it, might not
be entered even by the priests except for the high priest himself.
Once a year on a certain appointed day, bringing a more secret and
mystical sacrifice, he entered alone into the interior room. If such
distinctions were made in this Temple, which was a kind of image
and copy of the spiritual condition, the physical observance
teaches us that not all rational beings approach the Temple of God
(that is, the confession of the great God), but those who have
strayed to false beliefs are outside the divine enclosure. Moreover,
among those who have come inside by the strength of their

4   The typological interpretation of the Temple is derived from
     the Epistle to the Hebrews, chapters 8-10.

confession, those who have cleansed themselves in advance by purifications and chastity are honored more than the others; and among these, those who have dedicated themselves to the ascetic life already have the greater part, so that they are counted worthy to enter into the inner mysteries. It is possible to make the interpretation of the symbolism even clearer. We can learn these things by the teaching of the passage: some of the rational powers are seated like the holy altar in the inaccessible sanctuary of the Godhead; others again of them appear prominently, set in front like horns; and others around them are first and second according to some order of rank. The race of men, however, because of the evil which has entered us, has been driven outside of the divine precinct. Only those who are cleansed by the purifying bath[5] may come inside.

"Since at some time these middle partitions are going to be destroyed[6] (the partitions by which evil has shut us off from the sanctuary which is inside the curtain), when our nature will have its tabernacle pitched again by the resurrection, and all the corruption which has entered in connection with evil will be abolished from the things that are, then the festival around God will be inaugurated in common for those who are covered by the resurrection, so that one and the same joy will be set before all. No longer will rational beings be divided by different degrees of participation in equal good things. Those who are now outside because of evil will eventually come inside the sanctuary of divine blessedness, and will join themselves with the horns of the altar (that is, with the preeminent powers of the heavenly beings). The apostle says this more plainly, expounding the agreement of the universe in the good: 'To Him every knee will bow' of heavenly, earthly, and subterranean beings, and 'every tongue will confess that Jesus Christ is Lord to the glory of God the Father.'[7] Instead of horns he

5   Baptism.
6   Compare Ephesians 2:14.
7   Philippians 2:10-11; see above p. 63.

speaks of angelic and heavenly beings, and by the rest he signifies
the creatures which are ranked next after them, namely us, for all
of whom one harmonious festival will prevail. This festival is the
confession and knowledge of the One who truly is.[8]

"Furthermore, it is possible," she said, "to gather many other
testimonies from the holy Scriptures to support the doctrine of the
resurrection. Ezekiel, for example, leaping over the whole interval
of time and space by his spirit of prophecy, takes his stand at the
very moment of the resurrection by his power of foreknowledge.
As if already beholding that which will be, he brings it before the
view of his narration. He sees a vast plain extended without limit
and on it a great heap of bones, thrown about here and there
haphazardly. Then he sees them moved together by divine power
towards the bones which belong to them, and growing into their
own joints. Then sinews, flesh, and skin enwrap them (which the
psalm calls 'covering'), and a spirit gives life and awakens all that
were lying dead.[9]

"Why should one mention the apostle's enumeration of the
miracles connected with the resurrection, which is readily available for the reader? The passage tells how at a command and the
sound of trumpets, all together in a moment of time, those who are
lying dead will be changed into a condition of immortal nature.[10]
We shall also pass over the words of the Gospels, because they are
well known to everyone. The Lord does not merely say in words
that the dead will rise, but He brings about the actual resurrection,
beginning His wonder-working with those miracles which are
nearer to us and less likely to be disbelieved. First He shows His
life-giving power in mortal diseases, dispelling sufferings by His

8   In the Greek Bible, God's words in Exodus (3:14) "I am who
    I am" are translated as "the existing one." Philo of Alexandria
    associated this with Plato's philosophical expression for the
    divine, "that which truly is."
9   Ezekiel 37:1-14.
10 1 Corinthians 15:51-53.

word of command.[11] Then He wakes a newly-dead child.[12] Next He raises from the coffin a young man who is already being carried to the tombs and gives him back to his mother.[13] After this, when the dead Lazarus has already begun to decompose, after four days He leads him out living from the tombs, by the command of His voice bringing to life the man who was lying dead.[14] Then, when His own humanity has been pierced with nails and spear, He raises it from the dead on the third day, keeping the prints of the nails and the wound of the spear as evidence of His resurrection. Concerning these deeds I do not think it is necessary to go into detail, as there is no doubt among those who have accepted the Scriptures."

"But," I said, "this was not the question I was asking. For most of the hearers will agree on the basis of the scriptural proofs and the arguments already examined that the resurrection will take place at some time and that mankind will be subjected to the infallible judgment. We need to investigate whether that which is expected will be like that which is now. If it should be so, I would say that we human beings ought to shun the hope of the resurrection. For if our human bodies are reestablished in the next life just as they were when they departed from this life, then what we men hope for is an endless misfortune. What more pitiable sight could there be than when in extreme old age the shrivelled bodies become ugly and misshapen, when the flesh is used up by time and the wrinkled skin is dried to the bones? The sinews are contracted when they are no longer lubricated by the natural moisture, and because of this the whole body is drawn together and becomes an absurd and pitiable sight. The head is bent down to the knee, and the hand which has become useless for its natural operation is always shaking to and fro with involuntary spasms. Or what about the bodies of those who are

11 For example John 4:46-53, Luke 7:1-10.
12 Luke 8:49-56 and parallels.
13 Luke 7:11-17.
14 John 11:1-44.

wasted by chronic diseases, which differ only so much from bare bones as to appear covered by a thin and already worn-out skin? Or what about those who are swollen with dropsical illnesses? And what word could bring before our sight the shameful disfigurement of those subject to the sacred disease, how gradually as the decay progresses it eats away all their members, both the limbs used for action and the organs of perception?[15] What would one say about those mutilated in earthquakes or wars or from some other cause, who before their death live for some time in this unfortunate condition, or about those who from birth by some accident have grown up with distorted limbs? What can we think about the newly-born infants who are exposed or strangled[16] or perish by accident? If they are brought back again to life, will they remain in infancy? What could be more miserable? Or will they reach the measure of maturity? And by what milk will their nature nourish them?

"So if our bodies will be revived the same in all respects, what we expect is a misfortune; but if they will not be the same, the one who is being raised will be a different person from the one who was dead. For if the child has fallen, but the adult is raised, or vice versa, how can we say that the very one who was lying dead is raised up, if the fallen person appears at a different stage of life? If we see an adult instead of a child, and instead of an old man one in the prime of life, we behold a different person from the other. The same is true if we see a whole person instead of a cripple, and a robust person instead of an emaciated one, and all the other similar cases (I shall not make the discourse tiresome by going through each in detail). If the body does not return to life such as it was when it was mixed with the earth, it is not the dead body

15 The "sacred disease" is usually epilepsy, as in the Hippocratic writers, but here the reference is apparently to leprosy.
16 Infanticide was commonly practiced in the ancient world as a means of limiting family size.

which will be raised, but instead the earth will be fashioned again into another person. So what is the resurrection to me, if instead of me someone else will return to life? How would I myself recognize myself, seeing in myself that which is not myself? I would not truly be myself, if I were not in all respects the same as myself. It would be as if in the present life I had the image of someone in memory. Let us suppose for the sake of the illustration that the man has scanty white hair, protruding lips, a flat nose, pale skin, grey eyes, and a wrinkled body. In looking for this man, suppose that I should meet a young man with long hair, a hooked nose, dark skin, and all the rest of his appearance differing from the image in my memory: if I see someone like this, will I think that he is that man?

"But why should we spend time rather on the weaker objections, while we neglect the stronger? Who does not know that human nature is like a stream, proceeding from birth to death perpetually in motion and ceasing from motion only when it ceases from being? This motion is not any change of location, for our nature does not move out of itself but makes its progress through alteration. This alteration never remains in the same condition as long as it really is alteration; for how could the process of change be compatible with sameness? Our nature is like the fire on a wick which seems to be always the same because the continuity of its motion shows that it is inseparably united with itself, but in truth it is always replacing itself and never remains the same. For the moisture drawn out by the warmth at the same time blazes, burns up, and is changed into smoke. The movement of the flame is always energized by the power of change, converting the underlying matter into smoke by its activity. Thus, you see, even if you touch the flame again in the same place, you cannot take hold of the same flame twice.[17] The swiftness of the change does not wait for

17 According to Plato (*Cratylus* 402A), Heraclitus said, "You could not step twice into the same river." He also used imagery of fire to express the fluidity of apparently stable things.

you to touch it again a second time, no matter how quickly you do this, but the flame is always new and fresh, always new-born and never remaining in the same condition. Something like this happens also in regard to the nature of our bodies. The inflowing and outflowing of our nature which always proceed and move with the motion of change stop only when we cease from life. As long as our nature is alive, it has no stillness. Either the body is being filled or it is emptying itself, or actually it is always involved in both. So if a person is not the same as he was yesterday but becomes another by alteration, it follows that when the resurrection restores our body again to life, the one man will have to become a whole people. In this way no aspect of the one raised will be missing: the infant, the toddler, the child, the youth, the husband, the father, the old man, and all the intermediate stages.

"Since self-control and intemperance operate through the flesh, and since those who endure bitter punishments on behalf of true religion, as well as those who avoid them out of weakness, demonstrate each of these responses in their bodies, how can the judgment be just? If the same person now has sinned but again cleanses himself by repentance, and perhaps slips again into sin, so that the polluted body and the pure body alternate in the course of his life and neither one of them prevails throughout, what kind of body will be punished along with the licentious person? The body which is shrivelled with old age as it approaches death? But this is different from the one which perpetrated the sin. Or that which was polluted by passion? And then where is the elderly man? For either he will not rise, and the resurrection is not effective, or else he will be raised, and the guilty one will escape justice.

"Shall I also mention another of the objections which are made to us by those who do not accept the doctrine? 'Nature,' they say, 'has made no part of the body useless. The cause and power of our life reside in some parts without which our fleshly life cannot subsist, such as the heart, liver, brain, lungs, stomach, and the other internal organs. To other parts the impulse of perception is allotted. Others contain the active and motive energy, and others are appropriate for the procreation of successors. So if the life hereafter will subsist in the same functions, the change will be to no purpose. If, however, the word is true,' as indeed it is true, 'which declares that marriage will not be involved in the life after the resurrection nor will that life be maintained by food and drink,[18] what will be the use of those parts of the body, since the purposes for which the limbs are now adapted are not expected to persist in that life? If the organs of marriage exist for the sake of marriage, when that function does not exist we shall need none of the organs for that function. Similarly the hands are for work, the feet for running, the mouth for the reception of food, the teeth for the service of nourishment, the bowels for digestion, and the outlet passages for the elimination of what has been used. So when these functions do not exist, how or for what purpose will the organs which came to be because of them still exist? If there should not be any parts in the body which will not contribute towards that life, then logically none of the organs which now complete the body should exist; for our life would subsist in a different kind of body and we could no longer call such a state 'resurrection,' if all the individual members do not rise along with the body because they are not needed in that life. If on the other hand the resurrection will be effective through all of these organs, He who brings about the resurrection will be creating parts for us which are useless and meaningless for that life. But in fact we believe that there is a resurrection, and that it is not absurd. Therefore we must consider carefully how we can show the whole doctrine to be plausible."

When I had gone through all this, "Bravely," my teacher said, "you have attacked the doctrine of the resurrection by the art which they call rhetoric, persuasively surrounding the truth with destruc-

18 Matthew 22:30 and parallels; Romans 14:17.

tive words, so that those who have not adequately investigated the mystery of truth are likely to be affected by your speech and to suppose that you have validly raised a further difficulty in regard to what we have said. But this is not the truth," she said, "even if I am not able to orate against your speech in the same style. The truth about this is stored up in the hidden treasury of wisdom and will be disclosed at the time when we are taught the mystery of the resurrection in deed, when we will no longer need words to reveal what we hope for. If at night wakeful people discuss at length what the light of the sun is like, the grace of the rays by its mere appearance makes vain the verbal description; in the same way every reasoning which conjectures about the future restoration will be proved worthless when what we expect comes to us in experience.

"But since we should not leave entirely unexamined the objections brought against us, we shall take up their discussion in the following manner. First we must understand what the aim is of the doctrine about the resurrection, why this is declared by the holy revelation, and why we believe it. Therefore to describe this doctrine and limit it with a certain definition, we shall say this, that resurrection is the restoration of our nature to its original condition. In the first life, of which God himself became the creator,[19] there was presumably neither old age, nor infancy, nor the sufferings caused by the many kinds of diseases, nor any other type of bodily misery; for it is not likely that God created such things. Human nature was a divine sort of thing, before humanity started on the course of evil. All these things attacked us when evil entered our life. Therefore the life without evil will not need to be subject to the conditions which have happened because of evil. If a man travels through frosts his body inevitably becomes cold, or

19 For "creator," Macrina uses the word δημιουργός suggesting a contrast with the Demiurge of Plato's *Timaeus*, who fashions a less-than-perfect world.

if he goes through warm sunshine his face becomes dark. If, however, he should make his journey without either of these conditions, he would be freed entirely from the dark and the cold. No one could reasonably ask why this happened, when the cause of coldness or darkening is absent. In the same way, when our nature became subject to passions, it encountered those conditions which necessarily follow the life of passion; but when it returns again to the passionless blessedness, it will no longer encounter the consequences of evil. Since whatever was added to human nature from the irrational life was not in us before humanity fell into passion, we shall also leave behind all the conditions which appear along with passion.[20] If a man wearing a ragged tunic should be denuded of his garment, he would no longer see on himself the ugliness of what was discarded. Likewise, when we have put off that dead and ugly garment which was made for us from irrational skins (when I hear 'skins' I interpret it as the form of the irrational nature which we have put on from our association with passion), we throw off every part of our irrational skin along with the removal of the garment.[21] These are the things which we have received from the irrational skin: sexual intercourse, conception, childbearing, dirt, lactation, nourishment, evacuation, gradual growth to maturity, the prime of life, old age, disease, and death. If we will not be wearing that skin, how shall we preserve the conditions which come from it? So since we hope for a different state in the life to come, it is pointless to object to the doctrine of the resurrection because of what has nothing in common with that life. For if bodies with their changeable nature become shrivelled or robust, wasted or plump, or any other shape, what does this have to do with that life, which is

20 It is not clear how this version of man's creation agrees with that given above (p. 57), even if emotions are to be distinguished from passions.
21 Gregory's interpretation of Genesis 3:21. He is probably following Origen, for whom the "garments of skin" were a kind of denser materiality which bodies took on after the fall.

separated from the changing and transitory course of this life? The
principle of resurrection seeks one thing only, that a man has come
to be by generation, or rather, as the Gospel says, if a man has been
born into the world;[22] but length or shortness of life, and the
manner of death, whether it happened in this way or another, are
irrelevant when we are examining the principle of the resurrection. For whatever hypothetical circumstances we may imagine, it
is all the same, since such a difference makes neither difficulty nor
ease for the resurrection. He who has begun to live must undoubtedly return to life when the dissolution which interrupted his life
has been corrected by the resurrection. But how or when the
dissolution takes place, what does this have to do with the resurrection?

"The investigation of these matters aims at a different goal,
such as whether a person lived pleasantly or painfully, virtuously
or wickedly, whether he passed his time so as to deserve praise or
blame, in wretchedness or blessedness. All these and similar
questions are answered from the measure and character of one's
life. To evaluate the way a person has lived, the judge would need
to examine all these factors: how he endured suffering, dishonor,
disease, old age, maturity, youth, wealth, and poverty; how
through each of these situations he ran the course of the life
allotted to him either well or badly; and whether he became able
to receive many good things or many evil things in a long lifetime
or did not reach even the beginning of either good or evil, ceasing
to live when his mind was not yet fully developed. But when God
brings our nature back to the first state of man by the resurrection,
it would be pointless to mention such matters and to suppose that
the power of God is hindered from this goal by such obstructions.
He has one goal: when the whole fullness of our nature has been
perfected in each man, some straightway even in this life purified
from evil, others healed hereafter through fire for the appropriate

22 John 16:21.

length of time, and others ignorant of the experience equally of good and of evil in the life here, God intends to set before everyone the participation of the good things in Him, which the Scripture says eye has not seen nor ear heard, nor thought attained.[23] This is nothing else, according to my judgment, but to be in God Himself; for the good which is beyond hearing, sight, and heart would be that very thing which surpasses everything. But the difference between a life of virtue and a life of wickedness will appear hereafter chiefly in allowing us to participate earlier or later in the blessedness which we hope for. The duration of the healing process will undoubtedly be in proportion to the measure of evil which has entered each person. This process of healing the soul would consist of cleansing it from evil. This cannot be accomplished without pain, as we have discussed previously.[24]

"Truly, we should recognize the superfluity and ineptitude of the objections, as we plumb the depth of the apostle's wisdom. He explains this mystery to the Corinthians, who may perhaps also have made the same objections to him which are brought forward now by those who attack the doctrine to overthrow our faith. With his own authority he cuts short the audacity of their ignorance, speaking in this manner: 'Will you say to me, "How are the dead raised? With what kind of body do they come back?" Fool,' he says, 'what you sow does not come to life unless it dies; and what you sow is not the body which will be, but a bare kernel perhaps of wheat or some other grain. But God gives it a body as He has chosen.'[25] Here he seems to me to be reproving those who measure the divine power by their own strength, who think that only so much is possible for God as human understanding can comprehend and that what is beyond us exceeds God's power as well. For he who asks the apostle, 'How are the dead raised?' is asserting that the scattered

23 1 Corinthians 2:9, quoting Isaiah 64:4.
24 See above p. 84.
25 1 Corinthians 15:35-38.

elements of the body cannot come again into combination. Because
he supposes that this is impossible and that no other body exists
besides the combination of the elements, like a clever dialectician
by some sequence of reasoning he concludes what he assumed as
hypothesis. He says, 'If the body is a combination of the elements,
and if these cannot come together again a second time, what kind
of body will they use who rise?' So this argument, which these
people think they have constructed by some kind of clever wisdom,
the apostle calls the foolishness of those who have not seen in the
rest of the creation the surpassing greatness of divine power. He
leaves aside the more sublime of God's miracles, by which he
could have led the hearer into perplexity, such as, 'What is the
heavenly body, and where does it come from? What about the solar
and lunar bodies? Or the body which appears in the stars?[26] The
ether? The air? Water? Earth?' Instead he refutes the careless
objectors from familiar and common experiences. 'Does not
farming teach you,' he says, 'that a man is a fool if he evaluates
the surpassing greatness of the divine nature by his own measure?
Where do the seeds get the bodies which grow around them? What
leads to their sprouting? Is it not death, if indeed the dissolution
of a compound is a kind of death? The seed would not begin to
grow outwards if it were not dissolved in the soil and did not
become loose-textured and porous, so that its own quality could
be mixed with the surrounding moisture. It is transformed into
root and sprout, yet does not remain in these, but changes into a
stalk with joints in it like supporting braces to help it carry upright
the ear heavy with fruit. So where were these features of the grain
before its dissolution in the earth?' 'But they come from the seed.'
'If the seed did not come before, the ear would not begin to exist
afterwards. So you see, the body of the ear grows from the seed
when the divine Power creates the one from the other by art, and
the ear is neither altogether the same as the seed nor entirely
26 Compare 1 Corinthians 15:40-41.

different. In the same way,' he says, 'the mystery of the resurrection is already proclaimed to you in advance by the miracles accomplished in the seeds. The divine Power in the excess of Its might not only gives back to you that which was dissolved but also adds for you other great and beautiful gifts through which your nature is built up to greater magnificence. It is sown,' he says, 'in corruption; it is raised in incorruption; it is sown in weakness, it is raised in power; it is sown in dishonor, it is raised in glory; it is sown a physical body, it is raised a spiritual body.'[27] When the grain in the earth leaves behind after its dissolution the small quantity of its size and the particular quality of its shape, nevertheless it does not abandon itself. While remaining in itself it becomes an ear which differs completely from its former self in size, beauty, variety, and form. In the same manner the human nature also, when it abandons to death all the properties which it acquired through the state of subjection to passion (I mean dishonor, corruption, weakness, difference of age), does not abandon itself. Instead, as if ripening into an ear, it changes into incorruptibility, glory, honor, power, and every kind of perfection. It no longer has its life ordered by its natural properties, but goes over into a spiritual and immutable state (for it is characteristic of the physical body to be continuously altered from what it is and to be always changing into something different). Of those excellent qualities which we see now shared by human beings along with plants and animals, none will be left in the life hereafter.

"But I think that the apostolic word agrees with our idea of the resurrection and shows what our definition means when it says that the resurrection is nothing other than the restoration of our nature to its original state.[28] In the beginning of the creation we have learned from the Scripture that first the earth sprouted the plant of the grass, as the story tells, and then the seed came from the plant.

27 1 Corinthians 15:42-44.
28 See above p. 113.

When this fell on the earth, the same species as that which grew originally sprang up again.[29] The divine apostle says that this happens also at the resurrection. We learn from him not only that mankind changes to greater magnificence but also that what we hope for is nothing other than what was at first. Since in the beginning the ear did not come from the seed, but the seed from the ear, and after this the ear grew around the seed, the order of the symbolic narrative clearly shows that all the blessedness which will spring up for us through the resurrection will bring us back to the grace of the beginning. For we also were in some manner the ear at the beginning. When we are dried up by the hot summer of evil, the earth, which receives us dissolved by death, in the spring of the resurrection will reveal this bare seed of the body again an ear, large, abundant, upright, and reaching to the height of heaven, adorned not with a stalk or a beard but with incorruptibility and the rest of the godlike qualities; for he says, 'This corruptible nature must put on incorruptibility.'[30] Incorruptibility, glory, honor, and power, which are agreed to be characteristic of the divine nature, formerly belonged to the one made in God's image, and are expected to be ours once again. The first ear was the first man, Adam. Since at the entrance of evil our nature was split up into a multitude like the kernels in the ear, each of us, denuded of the form of that first ear and mixed with the earth, at the resurrection will spring up again in the archetypal beauty. Instead of the one first ear, however, we shall have become the innumerable myriads of the wheatfield. But the life of virtue will have this difference from the life of evil, that those who have tended themselves with virtue through their life here will grow at once into a perfect ear. Those, however, for whom the power in the physical seed has become weakened and wind-blasted through evil (like what the experts in these matters say

29 Genesis 1:11-12.
30 1 Corinthians 15:53.

happens to the seeds which are called 'horn-struck'),[31] even if they sprout in the resurrection, will receive severe treatment from the judge, because they were not strong enough to grow up into the form of the ear and to become that which we were before the seeds fell to earth. The farmer will heal the harvest by gathering the tares and thorns which have grown up along with the seed and taken all the power which should have nourished the roots. Because of these bastard plants the genuine seed has remained undeveloped and immature, smothered by the unnatural growth.[32] So when all that is illegitimate and alien has been plucked out from the nourishing grain and is eliminated, after the fire has consumed whatever is contrary to nature, then the nature of these people also will flourish and will ripen into fruit through this kind of treatment, receiving again after a long period of time the common form which was set upon us by God in the beginning.

"Blessed are they for whom the perfect beauty of the ears rises immediately when they sprout in the resurrection. I do not say this because a bodily difference will appear at the resurrection in those who have lived in virtue or wickedness, as if we thought that the one would be imperfect in body, but the other would have a perfect body. Rather, as the prisoner and the free man are both very much alike in body during their lives but differ greatly from each other in their experience of pleasure and pain, so I suppose we should reckon the difference between the good men and the evil men in the

31   Macrina seems to be showing knowledge of agriculture, but in fact her words sum up the two sources of Gregory's language. "Weakened"(ἐξίτηλος) and "horn-struck"(κερασβόλος) are rare words which occur in Plato (*Republic* 497B, *Laws* 853D). "Wind-blasted" (ἀνεμόφθορος) is a rare word which occurs in the Greek Bible (Hosea 8:7). "Horn-struck" refers to seeds that are too hard to germinate or cook properly, supposedly because of falling against the horns of the plow-ox (Plutarch, *Convivial Questions* 2.700C).

32   Matthew 13.24-30; see above pp. 58-59.

time hereafter. For the bodies which grow again from the sowing are said by the apostle to have their perfection in incorruptibility, glory, honor, and power; but if these qualities are diminished, it does not mean that the body which has grown suffers any physical mutilation. It undergoes rather a deprivation and alienation of all the qualities which are considered good. So since a person must undoubtedly have one of the complementary qualities, either good or evil, obviously when we say that someone does not have the good, we are showing without doubt that he has evil. With evil, moreover, there is no honor, nor glory, nor incorruptibility, nor power. So whoever does not have these qualities must inevitably have the opposite qualities: weakness, dishonor, corruption, and everything of this kind. As we have said earlier in our discourse, the passions resulting from evil become hard for the soul to get rid of, thoroughly mixed up with it, growing onto it, and closely united with it.[33] So when such things are cleansed and purified away by the treatment through fire, each of the better qualities will enter in their place: incorruptibility, life, honor, grace, glory, power, and whatever else of this kind we recognize in God Himself and in His image, which is our human nature."

33 See above p. 54.

Citations and Allusions

Index